A Debt I Cannot Pay

A Study of God's Plan to Save His People

ROBERT S. CHAMBERS

WESTBOW
PRESS®
A DIVISION OF THOMAS NELSON
& ZONDERVAN

WestBow Press books may be ordered through booksellers or by contacting:

WestBow Press
A Division of Thomas Nelson & Zondervan
1663 Liberty Drive
Bloomington, IN 47403
www.westbowpress.com
1 (866) 928-1240

Scripture quotations taken from the New American Standard Bible® (NASB), Copyright 1960, 1962, 1963, 1968, 1971, 1972, 1973, 1975, 1977, 1995 by The Lockman Foundation. Used by permission. www.Lockman.org

ISBN: 978-1-5127-8825-9 (sc)
ISBN: 978-1-5127-8827-3 (hc)
ISBN: 978-1-5127-8826-6 (e)

Library of Congress Control Number: 2017907452

Print information available on the last page.

WestBow Press rev. date: 5/24/2017

To Janet, my high school sweetheart, best friend, and beloved wife. Being the one who brought me to Christ, you patiently have stood by my side, helping me grow in the faith over all these years and making this book possible.

Contents

Preface

The task of writing a book is not something I take lightly. There are many questions that must be answered first, not the least of which is "who needs another book?" Certainly, the Bible is sufficient, and any worthwhile spiritual insight must be based on biblical teaching. Otherwise, it is useless at best or, even worse, harmful. So, what is my motivation for writing a book? The title really says it all: *A Debt I Cannot Pay*. Finally, I have grasped the enormity of the debt that Jesus paid to secure the path to eternal life for humankind. With that heightened awareness, it is no longer possible for me to neglect my responsibility to share this good news with those who have not embraced God's gracious gift. Moreover, I believe there are five good reasons why I am well suited to write about what God has done for us through Jesus Christ.

First, I have a passion for teaching the truth of the gospel. After many years of wearing the name of Christ, I finally get it. Souls are at risk. Heaven and hell are real, and what we believe does matter. To the extent I am able to help people understand the true nature of God, His relationship with humankind, what He has done for us, and why things are the way they are, I am adding value. This is particularly important because there are so many false teachings in the world today. My hope is this treatment of the subject will motivate readers to test their beliefs against the consistent message of the Bible.

Second, my religious background has taken me from the

doctrines and worship practiced in denominational Christianity to the teaching and patterns revealed by God through the inspired writings of the New Testament. Recognizing the inconsistencies between the two and submitting to God's way over my way was not an easy transition. Having been there and done that equips me to help lead people to a better way based on God's truth and revelation.

Third, I address the subject from the perspective of an analytic personality with the mind-set of an engineer and scientific researcher. I say that not to brag about my credentials but to account for the book's structured approach to the study of biblical truth. God's plan for humankind has been examined starting from the beginning, taking nothing for granted, developing the spiritual concepts from scratch, and trying to describe what God has done and explain why and how He did it. Often, these things are glossed over as a matter of blind faith without taking advantage of the insight revealed from all the scriptures. I believe the more we know, the better off we are—and the stronger our faith becomes.

The fourth reason I wrote this book was to communicate to my family and friends what I believe and why I believe it. Over the years, I have made significant changes in my religious beliefs and my life. I used to think religious details didn't matter as long as you loved God and believed in Jesus. I have learned that this is not true. God expects us to honor Him and treat Him as holy by submitting to His will. When we deviate from His teachings and patterns, we are usurping the authority of God and assuming we have the right to do so. That has never been true, and the Bible is filled with many examples of those who have opted to do so and suffered the consequences. To remain strong, we must own our faith, knowing what we believe and why we believe it.

Finally, I want to share my ideas about how to teach the gospel of Christ. The general flow through the ten chapters of the book systematically develops the essential ingredients needed to present God's plan of salvation. Care has been taken to provide sufficient background to appeal to those who are generally unfamiliar with the tenets of Christianity. In addition, there are specific chapters dealing in more detail with the subtleties arising from the roles of belief and baptism. These topics often become stumbling blocks in the pursuit of biblical truth. To make it easier for readers to follow the logical development of topics in each chapter of the book, scriptures are referenced and frequently quoted. This is a deliberate attempt to minimize the distraction created by having to stop repeatedly and look up each verse as it is cited within the text.

Our pursuit of truth must never end. We will continue to grow as long as we feed on God's Word. It is what distinguishes true disciples. My hope and prayer is this book will accomplish three things for the reader: (1) bring about a greater understanding of God's plan to save His people, (2) justify the importance of using all scripture to arrive at spiritual truth, and (3) convict hearts to submit to God's will even if it means giving up past beliefs based on the traditions and doctrines of men. May God soften our hearts and grant us the will to submit our lives to Him.

Acknowledgments

There are two men who have had a profound influence on my spiritual life. The first is W. N. (Bill) Jackson who preached and taught where we worshipped at the Southwest Church of Christ in Austin, Texas. A man of great intellect, Bill was a powerful preacher, teacher, writer, and debater who had a remarkable love for the Lord. He taught me the importance of studying the Bible.

The second man who impacted my life so deeply is George Carman. I met George when he came to preach at the Netherwood Park Church of Christ in Albuquerque, New Mexico. George ignited my passion for evangelism. I especially thank him for reviewing this manuscript. I am truly blessed to have known these faithful men of the Lord.

Finally, I would like to thank Ron Bland for the many teaching opportunities he has created by inviting others to hear the message of Jesus.

CHAPTER 1
Humankind and Our Unique Relationship to the Creator

To fully understand our relationship with God, we must return to the beginning. The very first verse in the very first book of the Bible, Genesis 1:1, states, "In the beginning, God created the heavens and the earth." That single verse establishes three important biblical principles:

1. Our physical universe has not always existed.
2. The heavens and earth and everything in them came into being by an act of creation.
3. The cause behind this creative act (the effect) is an entity called God.

These principles are supported by New Testament scriptures as well.

> In the beginning was the Word, and the Word was with God, and the Word was God. He was in the beginning with God. All things came into being through Him, and apart from Him nothing came into being that has come into being. (John 1:1–3)

From the context of Genesis 1 and John 1, it is abundantly clear that these verses are describing the absolute beginning of all physical things. This includes space, matter, and all associated forms of energy. Moreover, the terminology "in the beginning" establishes the start of a timeline that heretofore simply did not exist.

It should not be surprising that these are difficult concepts to grasp. After all, creation was a unique event attributed to the workings of God through an intervention that is no longer observable. Often overlooked is the fact that time itself is a created entity and has meaning only in the physical realm. To better comprehend this point, consider the natural description of moving objects. By definition, the speed of a body is simply the distance covered during some time span. For example, a car driven at thirty miles per hour travels a distance of thirty miles in one hour. In equation form, this generally can be written as the following:

$$speed = \frac{distance}{time}$$

The necessity of the physical entities of space, matter, and energy to support the existence of time can be seen by manipulating the previous equation to express time as a function of distance and speed:

$$time = \frac{distance}{speed} \begin{array}{l} \Rightarrow Space \\ \Rightarrow Matter \, \& \, Energy \end{array}$$

In this representation, time is defined by moving an object at constant speed over some prescribed distance. Since distance requires space to register a change in position, and since speed involves energy moving matter, by definition, we know that time is based on the existence of all three entities—space, matter, and energy. These are the fundamental quantities involved in the creation of the physical realm as described in Genesis 1:1 and John 1:1–3.

Additional support for the principles of creation is found

in Hebrews 11:3: "By faith we understand that the worlds were prepared by the Word of God, so that what is seen was not made out of things which are visible." This verse reveals that the physical universe and everything in it were not made out of visible things that were already present. In other words, our universe and its components have not always existed. Rather, all things came into existence out of nothingness (ex nihilo creation), and this all happened in response to the will and Word of God (fiat creation). These facts reveal some additional information about the cause responsible for the creation. First of all, God is not and cannot be some incredible physical being. This is because Hebrews 11:3 says, "What is seen was not made out of things which are visible." The visible universe was not made from or by existing visible things, and a physical creator would be limited to doing just that. If what is seen was not made out of visible things, then all had to arise from another realm—a realm controlled by God.

So, what is God? In John 4:24, Jesus gave a Samaritan woman the answer to that question. Jesus said God is a spirit. Indeed, a careful examination of Genesis 1:2 confirms that assertion, since the text states, "The Spirit of God was moving over the surface of the waters." Since everything came from God, and since God is a spirit, then the source of all physical things is a spirit residing in the spiritual realm. Being flesh and blood, it is relatively easy for us to grasp the concept of physical things through genuine life experiences recorded by our natural senses of hearing, seeing, tasting, touching, and smelling. However, being confined to the physical realm, there is no equivalent way for us to relate to something as abstract as a spirit. The spiritual realm of God is simply beyond our reach, existing independently and beyond the bounds of the physical universe. Hence, the Spirit of God encompasses, surpasses, and transcends our physical universe. God functions at a different level from a different domain, and in so doing, He supersedes all that humankind can and does know in every way. Our knowledge of the events of creation is the source of what little we are able to discern about the divine attributes of God. From this knowledge of creation, four important characteristics of God can be deduced.

First, God is eternal. This is true because He exists independently from all physical things, including time. Note that, in context, eternal does not mean a very long or infinite amount of time. This is a common misconception. Rather, eternity embraces the absence of time. Since it has been shown that time is a physical entity that had a beginning, and since God existed "before" (i.e., outside of) time itself, then God must exist beyond time in this spiritual realm associated with eternity. The Bible acknowledges this concept in Psalm 90:2: "Before the mountains were born Or You gave birth to the earth and the world, Even from everlasting to everlasting, You are God." Expressed another way, one might say God is the one who exists independently from physical things and thereby independently from time itself. This is the thought conveyed by the psalmist in saying "from everlasting to everlasting." God existed when there was no creation, and God will continue to exist when the creation is no more.

Second, God is omnipresent, meaning all present or present everywhere. There is no physical location in this universe beyond the reach of God. This logically must be true, for all physical things came out of the spiritual realm by the will of God. Therefore, God, as a spirit, functions in the spiritual realm that encompasses and transcends all that is physical.

> Where can I go from Your Spirit? Or where can I flee from Your presence? If I ascend to heaven, You are there; If I make my bed in Sheol, behold, You are there. If I take the wings of the dawn, If I dwell in the remotest part of the sea, Even there Your hand will lead me, And Your right hand will lay hold of me. (Ps. 139:7–10)

Third, God is omnipotent. That is to say God is all-powerful. Nine times in Genesis chapter 1, the text says "then God said," and it was immediately done. According to the will and power of God, the heavens and the earth, the seas, and all that is in them came into being (Exod. 20:11). This is why the prophet Jeremiah said, "Ah Lord GOD! Behold, You have made the heavens and the earth by Your great power and by Your outstretched arm! Nothing is too difficult for You" (Jer. 32:17). The power required to execute the vast creation is simply beyond our comprehension.

Fourth, God is omniscient or all-knowing. All things being the product of His creative acts means that God, the Creator, must have planned and designed our entire universe and its contents. This includes managing and executing the complexity of every detail as well as establishing and maintaining the natural laws governing its behavior. Hebrews 1:3 says, "And He is the radiance of His Glory and the exact representation of His nature, and upholds all things by the word of His power." This passage reveals that creation was executed through the Son of God, and He upholds and maintains all things. That means the Son of God is responsible for preserving the physical workings of the universe to sustain a consistent environment for our existence.

It is by the word of His power that all natural laws governing the universe are maintained. Gravity is always at work, momentum and energy are conserved, the laws governing thermodynamics and chemistry continue to apply, and so forth. Colossians 1:17 similarly says, "He is before all things, and in Him all things hold together." In holding all things together, the Son of God is seen to be actively engaged in the physical universe created for humankind. This effort requires knowledge and power transcending the bounds of everything that has ever physically existed. It is little wonder that the psalmist writes, "Great is our Lord and abundant in strength; His understanding is infinite" (Ps. 147:5).

By now, it should be clear that humankind has no hope of ever fully understanding or comprehending the essence of God. Our physical limitations are simply too great. The best we can do is to acknowledge and appreciate all that God has done. In fact, the way we define or identify God is through His role as the Creator. In preaching the gospel message to the Gentiles, this is exactly how the apostle Paul introduced Gentiles to the concept of God. Think about it. How else could this be done? Paul did so by identifying and defining God through His role as the one who created the heavens and the earth. When the people of Lystra attempted to worship Paul and Barnabas as gods, Paul confronted them, saying, "Men, why are you doing these things? We are also men of the same nature as you, and preach the gospel to you that you should turn from these vain things to a living God, who made the heaven and the earth and the sea and all that is in them" (Acts 14:15).

Similarly, Paul preached to those on Mars Hill in Athens.

> The God who made the world and all things in it, since He is Lord of heaven and earth, does not dwell in temples made with hands; nor is He served by human hands, as though He needed anything, since He Himself gives to all people life and breath and all things. (Acts 17:24–25)

God's identity resides in His role as the Creator.

Given this background, we can begin to appreciate the unique aspects of our human existence and our relationship to God, the Creator. Being a part of His creation, we were endowed with a physical form. Genesis 2:7 says, "Then the Lord God formed man from the dust of the ground." These raw materials provided the ingredients for our fleshly bodies, but we know it was not the substance of human bodies—what they were made from—that uniquely distinguished humankind. We know this because other things sprang forth from that same ground. Genesis 2:9 says, "And out of the ground the Lord God caused to grow every tree that is pleasing to the sight and good for food." In Genesis 1:24, the Bible states, "Then God said 'Let the earth bring forth living creatures after their kind,'" which included the cattle and creeping things and beasts of the earth. It also is true that humankind was made to be a living, animated entity. A continuation of Genesis 2:7 reveals that God "breathed into his nostrils the breath of life and man became a living being." As fantastic as that is, being so different from the inanimate parts of our universe, this still is not our most distinguishing feature. After all, God created other animated life forms, animals to fly above the earth, swarm in the waters, and creep and move across the dry land (Gen. 1:20–25).

Actually, it is in Genesis 1:27 that the destiny and heritage of humankind was sealed. In this passage, we learn that "God created man in His own image, in the image of God He created him; male and female He created them." But what does it mean to be made in God's own image or own likeness as Genesis 1:26 declares? Given that God has just been defined as the eternal, omnipresent, omnipotent, omniscient Being that willed the entire physical universe into existence, how could humankind possibly be considered to have been made like God? The answer to this question lies in understanding the full nature of Jesus Christ who was born of a woman some two thousand years ago.

In Philippians 2:5–7, Paul tells the Christians in Philippi to "have this attitude in yourselves which was also in Christ Jesus, who, although He existed in the form of God, did not regard equality with God a thing to be grasped, but emptied Himself, taking the form of a bond-servant, and being made in the likeness of men." Although the point of the text is to use the example of Jesus Christ to teach a lesson in humility, Paul does so by revealing what took place in the birth of Jesus. The Son of God, spoken of as the Word in John chapter 1, a Spirit, equal to and known as God (just as the Father and the Holy Spirit)—this Spirit of what is called the Son of God—emptied Himself, relinquishing His spiritual form and took the form of a bond-servant. In so doing, He was "made in the likeness of men". In other words, a divine Spirit inhabited the physical body we know as Jesus. By this process, a Spirit was said to be made like men.

With this background and explanation, we can understand what it means when Genesis 1:26–27 states that man was made in the image and likeness of God. This statement is the converse of what was cited in Philippians 2:7. The Genesis text depicts the same process in reverse as illustrated in Figure 1.

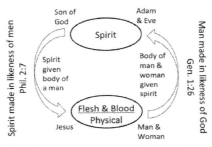

Figure 1. Humankind being made in the likeness of God is the reverse of what took place when the Son of God was made in the likeness of men.

In Jesus, a spirit was given a physical form of flesh and blood. In Adam and Eve, a physical form of flesh and blood was given a spirit. First Corinthians 2:11 is an excellent scripture acknowledging the dual nature of humankind—possessing both a physical body and a spirit. "For who among men knows the thoughts of a man except the spirit of the man which is in him? Even so the thoughts of God no one knows except the Spirit of God" (1 Cor. 2:11).

Among all life forms, only man and woman were said to be made in the image of God. This is true of no animal or other living thing, and this fact makes humankind unique among all God's creations. We alone possess a piece of God inside us. It is our spirit. By possessing this dual makeup, existing as both physical and spiritual beings, there is another profound implication. While it is true that our physical life will one day end when we die and return to the dust of the ground (Gen. 3:19), our spirit is eternal and will return to God (Eccl. 12:7). Having that common spiritual tie with our Creator provides the basis for an eternal relationship and ultimately explains the great lengths to which God goes to preserve that relationship and fellowship with humankind.

The consequences of possessing a spirit seem profound even in the physical realm. Genesis chapter 1 makes it clear that humankind was placed in an elevated position in the hierarchy of God's creation. The earth and all things around it and in it were prepared as the environment and dwelling place for humankind, the pinnacle of God's creation. Moreover, by God's command and authority recorded in Genesis 1:26, 28, humankind was commanded and empowered:

- to populate the earth
- to subdue it
- to rule over all other living creatures

This required humankind to possess other distinguishing godlike characteristics:

- intelligence: ability to think, plan, reason, make judgments
- appreciation for abstract concepts such as beauty, love, responsibility
- emotions: caring, joy, happiness, remorse

The inescapable conclusion is that humankind is unique among all creation. God made us that way through a spiritual bond to Himself. Our value does not arise from the attributes of our physical bodies. The color of our skin, our height, or our attractiveness may be different from one to another, but all of us are spirits encapsulated within a physical body of flesh and blood. As such, our true nature and identity reside in being an eternal spirit. It is important always to draw comfort from that fact. When the days are tough, when things are not going well, when you are feeling beaten up and trodden under foot by this world, no matter what anyone else may tell you or say about you, no matter how you may feel about yourself and your life, always remember that you share a special relationship with the eternal Creator of this universe. You are never forgotten. God knows you so well as to have numbered the very hairs on your head (Matt. 10:30).

In conclusion, if you remember only one thing from this chapter, let it be the fact that God wants you to know you are special!

No one can ever take that away from you. Moreover, that fact made you so important that the Son of God was willing to die for you. Why? How can it be? Those questions are answered in the chapters to follow. But first, where do we go to learn more about spiritual things? How can we discover the truth and know that we possess it? Those questions are addressed in chapter 2 by exploring the source of all spiritual truth.

CHAPTER 2

The Source of All Spiritual Truth

In the previous chapter, our relationship to the Creator was established by examining the nature of God and the nature of humankind. Genesis chapter 1 revealed that all physical things came from something spiritual. That something was a Spirit, called God. God willed into existence the entire universe and everything in it. However, unlike the other living creatures, God made humankind special, possessing not only a physical form of flesh and blood with a superior intellect but also a spirit, being made in the image and likeness of God (Gen. 1:26).

True human identity resides as a spirit, encapsulated within a fleshly body and currently dwelling in this physical realm. No doubt that spawns many other questions, so it seems only reasonable to determine how we can learn more about spiritual things. This presents a problem. Being flesh and blood, we are confined to the physical realm. Although humankind has been able to study and learn much about the physical creation by observation and experimentation, these approaches do not extend into the spiritual realm. On our own, spiritual truths are simply out of our reach—with one exception. That exception involves the knowledge of God. There are only two ways we can know anything about God and the spiritual realm. One way is through an examination of the creation itself, and the second way is if God chooses to reveal it to us.

First, consider how the creation itself reveals something about God.

> For the wrath of God is revealed from heaven against all ungodliness and unrighteousness of men who suppress the truth in unrighteousness, because that which is known about God is evident within them; for God made it evident to them. For since the creation of the world His invisible attributes, His eternal power and divine nature, have been clearly seen, being understood through what has been made, so that they are without excuse. (Rom. 1:18–20)

What is the cause attributed to the unrighteousness and ungodliness of these men? The text states it is because they suppressed the truth in unrighteousness. And what was the truth they suppressed? It was a knowledge of God that had been made evident to them through the creation.

Paul attested to the fact that the existence of God and His divine attributes of eternal power have been clearly seen and can be understood through what has been made. God has made Himself known to humankind through the existence of the universe and everything in it. The implication is clear. Being endowed with a superior intellect and the physical senses to observe and learn from the world around us, God expects us to process that information and draw the only rational conclusion possible.

The complexity and vastness of this universe—with all the intricacies of life in such a deliberate and delicately balanced environment—should be sufficient to convince humankind of the existence of an eternal, omnipotent, omniscient, omnipresent Creator (as was demonstrated in chapter 1). All these things just couldn't have happened by chance. It defies mathematical probabilities as well as common sense and reason. Moreover, the evidence for God found in the creation is so convincing that Paul claimed there is no excuse for anyone denying this truth. God will hold each one of us accountable for knowing Him as the Creator. In other words, no man or woman can ever credibly stand before God arguing, "I never knew You existed."

In the very beginning, God directed humankind to rule over the earth and subdue it (Gen. 1:26, 28). By authorizing us to take charge of the world, God provided the challenges that have embraced all productive human activities over the years, including:

- taking personal responsibility and exercising stewardship over all the things that God has given us,
- studying our world—the earth and all the life within,
- discovering the laws of nature that God has imposed on the universe, and
- harnessing the acquired knowledge for our common good.

By His directives to humankind, God effectively authorized the foundation of science and technology. This was a very practical and clever way for God to reveal Himself to humankind and be sure that we would get the chance to see Him. What better way than to dazzle us with such vastness, complexity, and delicate balance found in the existence of life and workings of the universe. As Psalm 19:1 says, "The heavens are telling of the glory of God; And their expanse is declaring the work of His hands."

Although the creation itself is evidence testifying to the existence of a Creator, it provides no specific information revealing other spiritual truths. It does not provide a way to get answers to spiritual questions that quite reasonably come to mind. Fortunately, however, because of our special relationship with the Creator, God cared enough to fulfill that need. That leads to the second way we know anything about God—namely, if He chooses to reveal it.

Has God communicated with humankind over the ages? If so, how did He do it? More importantly, how can we today get answers from God and know for certain that we possess the truth? These questions are addressed beginning in Hebrews 1:1–2 where the Bible says, "God, after He spoke long ago to the fathers in the prophets in many portions and in many ways, in these last days has spoken to us in His Son, whom He appointed heir of all things, through whom also He made the world."

God always has made His presence and His expectations known to humankind. In the beginning, through the age of the Patriarchs, God spoke directly to the fathers—men such as Adam (Gen. 2:16–17; 3:9–19), Noah (Gen. 6:13–21), and Abraham (Gen. 12:1–3). Later, God spoke through prophets such as Samuel (1 Sam. 3:21–4:1; 8:7–10), Jeremiah (Jer. 1), and Jonah (Jon. 1). His final revelation to us, however, was made during these last days through His Son "who, although He existed in the form of God, did not regard equality with God a thing to be grasped, but emptied Himself, taking the form of a bond-servant, and being made in the likeness of men" (Phil. 2:6–7). This passage describes the nature of Jesus as the incarnation of God wherein Jesus was empowered to speak to humankind on behalf of God, the Father. This fact was attested to and affirmed by God during the divine transfiguration of Jesus on the mountaintop in the presence of Peter, James, and John (Matt. 17:1–5). There Jesus was visually glorified with His face shining like the sun, His garments as white as light, and God's voice from the cloud proclaiming, "This is my beloved Son, with whom I am well pleased; listen to Him" (Matt. 17:5). It is also noteworthy, that throughout His ministry, Jesus acknowledged this fact over and over again, saying that His words were not His own but were from the Father who sent Him (John 12:49; 14:10, 24)

This is all well and good, but it does not explain how we, today, can access the same spiritual truths revealed by Jesus some two thousand years ago. After all, none of us were there to hear and see Jesus, and He has long ago departed physically from the earth. The answer lies in God's delegated plan of authority. Just as during His time on earth, Jesus was authorized by God to carry out the will of the Father and reveal God's truth to humankind, so it is that Jesus passed this authority and responsibility to a select group of men chosen to be His apostles.

Jesus addressed this in the Great Commission:

> All authority has been given to Me in heaven and on earth. Go therefore and make disciples of all nations, baptizing them in the name of the Father and the Son and the Holy Spirit, teaching them to observe all that I commanded you; and lo, I am with you always, even to the end of the age. (Matt. 28:18–20)

From His position of total authority, Jesus commanded His apostles to continue His work of making disciples and teaching them to observe everything He had taught them. The task of revealing God's Word to all humankind was to continue through the efforts of God's designated messengers.

On first hearing, this plan may actually sound a little foolish and beneath the wisdom of an omniscient God, for we know all too well the frailty and limitations of humankind. We suffer from faulty memories and are often driven by evil motives, pride, selfishness, envy, and the temptation to make followers for ourselves—any of which could corrupt the message and undermine God's purpose of revealing spiritual truths to humankind. It should come as no surprise that an omniscient God was well aware of the potential problems and did account for these things. In fact, this is one of those unique opportunities to peer into the mind of God and see how an omniscient Being anticipates and avoids potential problems.

To equip the apostles properly, Jesus promised to send them a Helper, the Holy Spirit or Spirit of Truth mentioned in John 14:16–17 and John 16:7. First of all, this was to provide these chosen men with a direct and perfect link to the Truth, the exact revelation from God, the Father. Jesus said, "But the Helper, the Holy Spirit, whom the Father will send in My name, He will teach you all things, and bring to your remembrance all that I said to you" (John 14:26).

> But when He, the Spirit of Truth, comes, He will guide you into all the truth; for He will not speak on His own initiative, but whatever He hears, He will speak; and He will disclose to you what is to come. He will glorify Me; for He will take of Mine, and will disclose it to you. All things that the Father has are Mine; therefore I said, that He takes of Mine, and will disclose it to you. (John 16:13–15)

This provided assurance that the message proclaimed by the apostles was the exact Word of God.

The second need fulfilled by the Holy Spirit was the ability to confirm the message and authenticate the messengers. There had to be some way to prove to all hearers that these words really came from God and not just from the minds and hearts of deceptive men. That need was satisfied by the miraculous signs and wonders executed by the apostles. The writer in Hebrews 2:3–4 confirms that God Himself bore witness. There the text states: "After it was at the first spoken through the Lord, it was confirmed to us by those who heard, God also testifying with them, both by signs and wonders and by various miracles and by gifts of the Holy Spirit according to His own will." Since God is responsible for the creation and He sustains all natural laws, only God is capable of suspending those laws. Hence, when the apostles performed supernatural events like raising the dead (Acts 9:36–41; 20:7–12), healing the lame (Acts 3:1–8; 14:8–10), and other miraculous signs and wonders (Acts 5:12, 16), such things could only be done through the blessing and power of God. The same power that confirmed the identity and message of Jesus through the miracles He performed was now being employed to endorse the work and teachings of the apostles.

As expected, the apostles attributed their knowledge of the truth directly to the Holy Spirit.

> For to us God revealed them through the Spirit; for the Spirit searches all things, even the depths of God. For who among men knows the thoughts of a man except the spirit of the man which is in him? Even so the thoughts of God no one knows except the Spirit of God. Now we have received, not the spirit of the world, but the Spirit who is from God, so that we may know the things freely given to us by God, which things we also speak, not in words taught by human wisdom but in those taught by the Spirit. (1 Cor. 2:10–13)

Paul attributed the words He spoke to a divine link to God through the Holy Spirit. Moreover, this is exactly how it was perceived by the people who heard the apostle's teaching.

> For this reason we also constantly thank God that when you received the Word of God which you heard from us, you accepted it not as the word of men, but for what it really is, the Word of God, which also performs its work in you who believe. (1 Thess. 2:13)

Although this establishes the fact that the apostles were miraculously empowered to continue the task of spreading God's truth, it does not yet answer the question of how we access that same information today. After all, the original, inspired apostles also passed away nearly two thousand years ago. While this is true, the Word of God has survived through their inspired writings. These men preached the message, and they wrote it down. In 2 Thessalonians 2:15, Paul told the Thessalonians to "stand firm and hold to the traditions which you were taught, whether by word of mouth or by letter from us."

By the traditions and teaching of inspired prophets, the Truth was shared verbally and through the written Word. Paul made a similar point in 1 Corinthians 14:37: "If anyone thinks he is a prophet or spiritual, let him recognize that the things which I write to you are the Lord's commandment." Moreover, these writings were deemed so important that they were read and circulated among the first-century church. In 1 Thessalonians 5:27, the apostle Paul commanded the Thessalonians: "I adjure you by the Lord to have this letter read to all the brethren." Note also Paul's instructions in Colossians 4:16: "When this letter is read among you, have it also read in the church of the Laodiceans; and you, for your part read my letter that is coming from Laodicea."

Today, we have access to God through the writings of the apostles and the other inspired prophets of God, just as Hebrews 1:1–2 declared. These scriptures are inspired by God. They are God breathed or out of the mouth of God. Second Peter 1:20–21 states, "But know this first of all, that no prophecy of scripture is a matter of one's own interpretation, for no prophecy was ever made by an act of human will, but men moved by the Holy Spirit spoke from God."

The intent of God's revelation to humankind is stated clearly by the apostle Paul in 2 Timothy 3:16–17: "All scripture is inspired by God and profitable for teaching, for reproof, for correction, for training in righteousness; that the man of God may be adequate, equipped for every good work." God knows we have questions about spiritual things and the meaning of life. He gave us the scriptures to provide answers to those questions and to prepare us for every good work in righteousness before Him.

We have been armed with the spiritual truth needed to teach, reprove, correct, and train ourselves and others to be pleasing and acceptable to God. Through the written Word, God has made His expectations known, and one of those expectations is for us to study that written Word and learn it. Note the instructions that Paul gave to the evangelist Timothy: "Be diligent to present yourself approved to God as a workman who does not need to be ashamed, handling accurately the Word of Truth" (2 Tim. 2:15).

To be an approved workman before God, we must handle the Word of Truth accurately. That requires study and a willingness to submit to the will of God. It is God's intent that we "contend earnestly for the faith that was once for all handed down to the Saints" (Jude 3). Since this Truth was delivered "once for all" to the saints in the first century, that means God's revelation to humankind is complete. There is simply no need for further instruction since what we have equips us for every good work according to 2 Timothy 3:16–17.

Because the scriptures are inspired by God, we are told repeatedly not to add to, take away from, or alter the message. We simply do not have that right.

> I testify to everyone who hears the words of the prophecy of this book: if anyone adds to them, God will add to him the plagues which are written in this book; and if anyone takes away from the words of the book of this prophecy, God will take away his part from the tree of life and from the holy city, which are written in this book. (Rev. 22:18–19)

The apostle Peter also warned of the seriousness of tampering with the Word. He called out those who are untaught and unstable for distorting Paul's letters and the rest of scriptures noting that this was said to be to their own spiritual destruction (2 Pet. 3:16). The apostle Paul put it even stronger saying, "But even if we, or an angel from heaven, should preach to you a gospel contrary to what we have preached to you, he is to be accursed" (Gal. 1:8). For emphasis, Paul repeated the same thought in the following verse: "If any man is preaching to you a gospel contrary to what you received, he is to be accursed." God's Word is immutable and unchangeable representing the "faith which was once for all handed down to the saints" (Jude 3).

By now, it should be clear that God alone is the source of all spiritual truth, and He has made that truth accessible to all humankind for all time through the written Word of the Bible. That means our source for spiritual authority today is not found among friends, family, preachers, church leaders, university professors, denominational creeds, synods, or religious councils. Jeremiah the prophet put it this way: "I know, O Lord, that a man's way is not in himself; Nor is it in a man who walks to direct his steps" (Jer. 10:23).

If we are all incapable of directing our own steps, how can we possibly direct the steps of others? We must not fall into the trap of relying on the flawed word of a middleman to know what God wants for us. Notice Paul even commended the Bereans for being more noble-minded than the Thessalonians because they received the Word with great eagerness, and they examined the scriptures daily to see whether these things were true (Acts 17:10–11). A spiritual message always should be checked against the holy scriptures of the Bible.

It is also important to remember that our emotions and feelings do not determine what is right before God. He emphasized that fact through the prophet Isaiah:

> "For My thoughts are not your thoughts, Nor are your ways My ways," declares the Lord. "For as the heavens are higher than the earth, So are My ways higher than your ways, And My thoughts than your thoughts." (Isa. 55:8–9)

We are simply incapable of anticipating the mind and will of God based on our own reasoning, thoughts, and feelings.

Finally, we must also remember that the human conscience cannot be trusted as our assurance of pleasing God. Our conscience must be trained, and it can be seared (1 Tim. 4:1–2). Proverbs 16:25 states, "There is a way which seems right to a man, But its end is the way of death." To rely on our own feelings or conscience as the gateway to truth can lead to spiritual death.

In summary, only God can speak for God. We must be willing to seek out His spiritual truths, which are freely available to all humankind through the Bible. By studying the Word for ourselves, we can know the truth and be equipped properly to live righteous lives before God and teach others through the written Word. This is the method by which God has chosen to reveal Himself to humankind, and it is the basis for everything that will be presented in this book. No wonder Paul tells Christians to put on the full armor of God, calling the Word of God the sword of the Spirit (Eph. 6:17). However, like any other weapon, our spiritual sword (the Word of God) can be misused. Chapter 3 provides a brief overview of the Bible, discussing its design and organization along with a few recommendations for how best to use it.

CHAPTER 3
A Brief Overview of the Bible

God has revealed Himself to humankind through the writings and teachings of the inspired prophets, and these works are available to us today through the pages of the Bible. The word *Bible* comes from a Greek word that means *books*. The Bible is actually a collection of books penned by many inspired authors over about 1,500 years. Because of that, it really is appropriate to think of the Bible as a library of sorts, authored by God through the miraculous direction of His Spirit. In fact, evidence for the authenticity of the Bible comes from its accuracy, consistency, and unity of message despite passing through the hands of so many men across generations. To use the Bible as God truly intended, however, it is important to understand the content and some things about the setting and organization of the writings.

The modern English Bible is divided into two major sections: the Old Testament and the New Testament. The term *testament* comes from a Greek word that might be translated better as *contract* or *covenant*. The basic idea is that, over the course of time, God made two different covenants with His people—and the New Covenant replaced the Old.

The Old Covenant dominates the thirty-nine books of the Old Testament, and in today's English Bibles, these books are arranged and often classified in the following groups:

- The five books of law (Pentateuch): Genesis, Exodus, Leviticus, Numbers, and Deuteronomy
- The twelve books of history: Joshua to Esther
- The five books of poetry: Job, Psalms, Proverbs, Ecclesiastes, and the Song of Solomon
- The five major prophets: Isaiah, Jeremiah, Lamentations, Ezekiel, and Daniel
- The twelve minor prophets: Hosea to Malachi

When applied to the books of the prophets, the terms *major* and *minor* do not indicate any difference in their importance. They all come from God and are inspired by Him. Rather, it merely refers to the fact that the books of the major prophets are larger in size than the books of the minor prophets. This ordering in the English Bible comes from the Latin Vulgate translation, which is derived from the Septuagint (Greek version of the Old Testament).

The twenty-seven books of the New Covenant often are organized in four New Testament groups:

- The four gospels: Matthew, Mark, Luke, and John (These books actually document events occurring under the Old Covenant but are included in the New Testament because they contain a description of the life of Jesus.)
- The one book of church history: Acts
- The twenty-one epistles (letters): Romans to Jude
- The one book of prophecy: Revelation

The first three gospel books—Matthew, Mark, and Luke—are known as the *Synoptic gospels* because of their similar contents. In all probability, the book of John was written at a later date. The first thirteen Epistles (Romans through Philemon) are attributed to the apostle Paul. Among those books, 1 and 2 Timothy and Titus are called the *pastoral epistles* by some. The author of Hebrews is a bit uncertain. Although its inspiration is not in question, some claim Paul is the author, and others believe it is someone else. James, 1 and 2 Peter, 1, 2 and 3 John, and Jude are known as the seven *general epistles.*

The original inspired Bible manuscripts were written in three languages: Hebrew, Aramaic, and Greek. The Hebrew and Aramaic languages are still spoken today in Israel and Syria, respectively. However, the Greek language spoken in Greece is quite different from the language of the New Testament. Almost all thirty-nine Old Testament books were written in Hebrew, which is one of a large family of languages known as Semitic languages. It is written from right to left and has twenty-two consonants with no vowels. Because of that, it has sounds quite different from spoken English and uses a vocabulary that is unrelated to English words.

Aramaic is a kindred language to Hebrew. It became the language of the common man in Palestine after the time of the Babylonian exile around 500 BC. Nehemiah 8:8 usually is understood to mean that the people did not know pure Hebrew and needed a translation into the more familiar Aramaic. In the centuries prior to the time of Jesus, Aramaic was spoken by the Jews, which led to some portions of the Old Testament being written in Aramaic rather than Hebrew. The New Testament scriptures actually contain quotes of Jesus using Aramaic. Matthew 27:46 says, "Eli, Eli Lama Sabachthani," which is Aramaic for "My God, My God, why hast thou forsaken Me?" On other occasions, such as Mark 14:36, Jesus addressed God as "Abba" (Aramaic for Father). Although Jesus actually spoke in Aramaic, the original New Testament manuscripts were written in Greek. During the first century, Greek was to the world much like English is today—the closest thing to a worldwide, common language that could be understood by all. Specifically, it was Hellenistic or Koine (common) Greek.

The Bible describes events spanning the time from the creation up through the establishment and early years of the church in the first century. Over this time frame, God dealt with humankind in different ways as the relationship and knowledge of Him grew. In a similar fashion, one might compare this to how a parent deals with a child as that child grows from infancy to adulthood. Consequently, when the Bible is read, it is important to pay particular attention to the context, noting the people, setting, and time period under consideration. This information is essential for determining the proper meaning of the text and what is applicable to us today. In general, the biblical timeline encompasses three ages or dispensations:

- The Patriarchal Age (Dispensation)
- The Mosaic Age (Dispensation)
- The Christian Age (Dispensation)

The Patriarchal Age is the first dispensation, and it began at the time of creation. The word *patriarch* refers to the "father" or head of a family. During this dispensation, God spoke directly to the patriarchs (fathers), communicating His expectations and empowering these men with the authority to teach and lead their families according to God's will. Under this system, families relied on the oral message from God communicated through the fathers because they had no written revelation to follow. Centuries later, the history of this time period was recorded for us, and it now can be found in the Old Testament scriptures starting in Genesis chapter 1 and extending to Exodus chapter 20. The latter chapter typically is associated with the beginning of the Mosaic Age.

The characters and stories from the Patriarchal Dispensation are rich in revealing much about the nature of God and humankind and the historical background and promises giving rise to God's chosen people. A subjective chronological summary of some of the key people and stories from this period might include the following:

- the creation of the heavens and earth and the first couple (Adam and Eve)
- the temptation of the forbidden fruit and the sinful fall of man in the Garden of Eden orchestrated by the devil acting through the serpent
- the first murder when Cain killed his brother Abel
- the Flood account whereby God destroyed an earth filled with evil, sparing only some of the animals, Noah, and his family through the ark
- the Tower of Babel where God confused the language to undermine an arrogant people who defied God's will to go forth and fill the earth
- the covenant with Abram promising an elderly, barren couple that they would produce a mighty nation from whom all the world would be blessed
- the story of Hagar, the maid of Sarai (later renamed Sarah), giving birth to Abram's child whom they named Ishmael
- the renaming of Abram to Abraham with God giving circumcision as a sign of the covenant
- the destruction of Sodom and Gomorrah as a people who rejected godliness
- the birth of Isaac and Abraham's test of faith by his willingness to obey God even to the point of sacrificing his own son, the promised heir
- Isaac's marriage to Rebekah and the birth of their sons, Jacob and Esau
- God's blessing for Jacob, renaming him Israel, and granting him twelve sons
- Jacob's favorite son, Joseph, falling into conflict with his brothers and being sold as a slave in Egypt
- Joseph, while serving Potiphar, the captain of Pharaoh's bodyguard, being falsely accused by Potiphar's wife and sent to prison

- Joseph rising to second in command of all Egypt after interpreting Pharaoh's dreams
- the great famine, which led to Joseph being able to reunite with his family and save them from starvation by bringing them to live in the land of Egypt
- the blessings of God extended to the sons of Israel (Jacob) and through their offspring producing the twelve tribes of God's chosen nation of Israel
- the rise of a new Egyptian pharaoh who perceived a threat from the foreigners in his midst and forced the Jews into slavery
- the birth of baby Moses whom God protected and groomed to become a deliverer for Israel
- the confrontation between Moses and Pharaoh, where God intervened with ten plagues upon Egypt after Pharaoh repeatedly refused to let the Jews go free
- God establishing the feast of the Passover for the Jews during the tenth plague, bringing death to all the firstborn of the Egyptians while passing over the people of Israel
- Pharaoh chasing the Jews to the shores of the Red Sea only to witness the waters parting with Moses leading the people to safety as the waters collapsed on the Egyptian solders in pursuit
- Moses leading the Jewish people into the wilderness of Sinai

At this point in the timeline, there is the beginning of a new dispensation, which is known as the Mosaic Age or Mosaic Dispensation. Just as the term suggests, it is associated with the Old Law or Old Covenant established with the nation of Israel and delivered to the people by God through Moses. The Mosaic Age covers the time frame from the giving of the Law of Moses to the establishment of the church around AD 30. During this period, God spoke to the people through inspired prophets, and over time, these prophets wrote down the things God revealed to them, providing us with the books of the Old Testament. Within the English Bible, the events of the Mosaic Dispensation are documented in the books from Exodus chapter 20 up through the second chapter in Acts. This includes the bulk of the Old Testament as well as the early part of the New Testament. The gospels and first two chapters of Acts are actually included under the Mosaic Dispensation because, during His lifetime on earth, Jesus lived as a Jew under the Mosaic Law. It was only after His death and resurrection that the New Covenant and Christian era began.

The chronology of the Mosaic Age begins with God making a covenant through Moses with the nation of Israel on Mount Sinai. Shortly after that, God directed Moses to send twelve men to spy out the promised land that God was to give them. When the spies returned, ten of the twelve presented a fearful report, questioning the ability of God's people to vanquish such mighty foes. For that lack of faith in God, the nation was sentenced to forty years of wandering in the wilderness. Death took its toll, making Caleb and Joshua the only adults permitted to enter the promised land. When Moses died, Joshua took over command and led Israel across the Jordan into the promised land, taking the city of Jericho as the walls came tumbling down.

Following the death of Joshua came the period of the Judges, where the nation functioned more as twelve separate tribes, undergoing cycles of being faithful to God and then becoming unfaithful again. Periodically, leaders arose from among their midst to save the nation from foreign oppression. These leaders were known as judges and included people like Gideon, Deborah, and Samson. Samuel, being the last judge, served as a transitional figure appointing the first earthly king of the nation at the request of a people who rejected the wise counsel of God.

The period of the Kings began with Saul and included the famous defeat of Goliath, the Philistine giant, who was dispatched by the sling of a young shepherd boy named David. David went on to become the next king, but then he fell into a sinful union with Bathsheba, ultimately ordering the death of her husband, Uriah, after David's futile attempts to cover up his affair and the conception of a child.

Solomon, the heir to David's throne, become the wisest man who ever lived, being granted his request for wisdom in response to a humble prayer out of concern about leading God's people. He also built the magnificent temple that David was not allowed to construct. When Solomon's son, Rehoboam, rejected sound advice and overburdened his people, the kingdom divided into two nations. Rehoboam became king of the tribes of Judah and Benjamin, ruling over the southern kingdom, Judah, with Jerusalem as its capital. Jeroboam ruled over the remaining ten tribes in the northern kingdom, Israel. Samaria eventually became the chief city.

The history of the northern kingdom encompasses many well-known Bible characters. The wicked King Ahab and Queen Jezebel were among the most notorious. There also were prophets such as Elijah, Elisha, Hosea, Amos, and Jonah, who was taught a lesson from the belly of a large fish. Ultimately, the Assyrians conquered the northern kingdom by about 722 BC. The people were carried into captivity and assimilated into a mixed population. This produced the Samaritans who were spurned by the pure-blooded Jews.

The southern kingdom of Judah had its noteworthy characters too. King Hezekiah resisted the Assyrians, and King Josiah was known as the great reformer. There were the well-known prophets Joel, Isaiah, and Jeremiah as well as Daniel who survived the lions' den. The southern kingdom eventually was taken captive by the Babylonians during the reign of King Zedekiah about 586 BC. Since the Jewish exiles from the southern kingdom were allowed to have their own settlements, they did not lose their identity like the Samaritans did.

The Babylonian empire eventually was replaced by the Medes and Persians. King Cyrus allowed the Jews to return to Jerusalem to rebuild the temple. In 445 BC, the Persian King, Artaxerxes I, gave Nehemiah permission to rebuild the city of Jerusalem. It was during this time that the prophet Ezra sought to restore the people's faith through the Law of Moses. By then, the Hebrew language was becoming less the language of common use. Most Jews outside Judea spoke Aramaic or Greek by the New Testament times.

From secular history, it is known that Alexander the Great conquered the Persian Empire and inaugurated a period of Greek rule from 336–323 BC. After his death, the empire broke into smaller empires ruled by his generals. Eventually, a Seleucid king defeated the armies of Egypt and took possession of Palestine, including Judea. When the king attempted to make political appointments to the Jewish high priesthood, plundered the Temple, and erected an altar to a pagan god, the devout Jews were outraged. This led to the Maccabean revolt with the Jews eventually winning independence to manage their own affairs and cleanse the Temple.

In about 63 BC, the Romans took control of the whole region. King Herod came to power in 37 BC. During his reign, Jesus Christ was born. As noted earlier, Jesus was born a Jew and lived His life under the Mosaic Dispensation. Through His ministry to the Jewish people, He taught about the coming kingdom of heaven (Matt. 4:17). Being the Son of God, Jesus lived a perfect life and revealed the nature and will of God to those who would hear. By His sacrifice on the cross, salvation was offered to all humankind.

This brings us to the third and final dispensation, the Christian Dispensation, marking the arrival of that coming kingdom through the creation of the church. For centuries, the Jewish people had been waiting for the arrival of the Anointed One. The Messiah would sit on the throne of David, according to the prophecies found in 2 Samuel 7 and Isaiah 9:6–7. On the day of Pentecost, the apostle Peter confirmed that this was Jesus, the Christ (Acts 2:36).

Through the church, God established a New Covenant with humankind, replacing the Old Covenant, which had been made with the nation of Israel. One of the distinguishing features about the Old Covenant was the fact that the Old Covenant was made only with the nation of Israel. Exodus 19:1–7 chronicles the giving of the Old Law to Israel on Mount Sinai.

In Deuteronomy 5:1–5, Moses refers to this covenant as having been given to all Israel not to their fathers. Years later, Jeremiah prophesied that the Old Covenant would be replaced with a New Covenant.

> "Behold, days are coming," declares the LORD, "when I will make a new covenant with the house of Israel and with the house of Judah, not like the covenant which I made with their fathers in the day I took them by the hand to bring them out of the land of Egypt, My covenant which they broke, although I was a husband to them," declares the LORD. "But this is the covenant which I will make with the house of Israel after those days," declares the LORD, "I will put My law within them and on their heart I will write it; and I will be their God, and they shall be My people. "They will not teach again, each man his neighbor and each man his brother, saying, 'Know the LORD,' for they will all know Me, from the least of them to the greatest of them," declares the LORD, "for I will forgive their iniquity, and their sin I will remember no more." (Jer. 31:31–34)

In the New Testament era, the apostle Paul, who also was a Jew, wrote in Ephesians 3:1–7, making it clear that this New Covenant was open to all humankind, both Jews and Gentiles alike. Paul said, "to be specific, that the Gentiles are fellow heirs and fellow members of the body, and fellow partakers of the promise in Christ Jesus through the gospel." The apostle Peter also attested to this fact in his remarks at the conversion of the Gentile Cornelius and his family recorded in Acts 10:34–36. Because this final dispensation is based on the sacrifice of Jesus, it usually is associated with the establishment of the church on the day of Pentecost.

The biblical record of the Christian Dispensation is contained in the New Testament books, starting at Acts chapter 2 and continuing through rest of the New Testament, ending with the book of Revelation. The gospels and first chapter of Acts are included in the New Testament because they describe the birth, ministry, and sacrifice of Jesus, the Christ, who is the founder of the Christian Dispensation.

Hopefully, this brief overview has provided sufficient awareness of the organization and content of the Bible to appreciate the use of scripture in the material offered in the chapters that follow. This is particularly important when it comes to understanding how to apply biblical teachings to our individual lives. One of the most common ways that the Bible is misused is by taking a passage out of context and applying a specific teaching to those for whom it was not intended. We must always be careful to understand to whom the passage is being written and under what dispensation or setting the passage is given.

While there are many teachings and lessons that apply across all ages/dispensations, there are some that do not. One example is the offering of animal sacrifices, which was part of the Patriarchal and Mosaic Ages but is no longer commanded in the Christian era. Another comes from worship practices under the Law of Moses that were designated only for the nation of Israel. These ended with the onset of the Christian Age. Since today all live in the Christian Dispensation, we must focus on the teachings and expectations that God has revealed to us in these last days through His Son (Heb. 1:2). That is the way for us to learn how to live a righteous life before God in this day and age. Also, it is where we discover the truth about salvation and the church, including what God intended for its organization, mission, doctrine, and worship.

We are now equipped with the spiritual tool needed to understand the challenging aspects of our spiritual nature. Probably the most obvious question is "Why should we care?" We possess a physical body of flesh and blood living in a well-defined environment on the earth. That fact is readily apparent to us all. Moreover, physical life can be productive, meaningful, and pleasurable. Isn't that enough? In contrast, the whole thought of spiritual things is foreign and abstract to us. It is, after all, unnatural by definition since it embraces another realm—the spiritual realm. So, why bother or worry about it? To answer these questions, it is important to consider the problem of sin. That is the subject of chapter 4.

CHAPTER 4
The Problem of Sin

The fact that God created humankind in His own image and likeness to have not just a physical body but to be endowed with an eternal spirit is something hard for us to grasp. We are quite familiar with physical things because each one of us has to deal with the harsh realities of life. This includes concerns for food, shelter, and clothing as well as coping with health, education, family, and jobs. Such things are easy for us to relate to because we experience them in a real way each day of our lives.

Our spirit and the spiritual aspect of our being are much more difficult for us to comprehend because the notion of a spirit is such an abstract concept to a physical being. Remember, the only way we even know about the existence of such things is through the revelation of God. And yet, just because we struggle with the concept does not make our spirits any less important or real. The truth and reality of our spiritual nature do not depend on our knowledge and understanding. Something isn't made false or insignificant just because we are unaware, uninformed, or don't understand it. In fact, our spirit and the existence of the spiritual realm are actually much more important to us than anything in the physical world. Most people just don't realize it. Chapter 4 is devoted to discovering why that is true.

To establish the importance of spiritual things, we first must reconsider the nature of God. In chapter 1, the divine attributes of God were deduced based upon the work of creation. That led to the understanding that all physical things came from something spiritual and that something was God, an eternal, all-present, all-knowing, all-powerful spiritual being. Although this provides us with some insight into God's capabilities, it tells us nothing about the character or personality of God. That information must be determined by what God has revealed to us through the written word of the Bible. That source of spiritual truth was discussed in chapter 2.

The Bible unequivocally describes God as a benevolent being, portraying every quality of what is associated with moral goodness, love, virtue, righteousness, and justice. The Psalms praise God using many words to describe His nature:

- good, righteous, gracious, merciful, loving, kind, and patient (Psalm 145)
- faithful, just, and truth (Psalm 89)

In the New Testament, the Bible describes God as love (1 John 4:16) and calls Him a God of "light" in whom "there is no darkness at all" (1 John 1:5). God is the standard of perfection. These traits established the moral code for our civilized society. As wholesome as these qualities are, they still do not capture the essence of what makes the nature of God so unique. That uniqueness comes from the fact that God is said to be "holy" (Lev. 19:2; 1 Pet. 1:15–16; Rev. 4:8).

Holy is one of those religious words that we associate with God, but we often have a hard time defining it. Sometimes the same thing is expressed by using other obscure words like *sanctified*, *consecrated*, or *sacred*. What do these words really mean? The biblical concept of a "Holy God" means God is *set apart*, *distinct*, *dedicated*, and *totally pure*. In practical terms, it means God is one-sided, being solely a benevolent being, characterized by all the previously defined qualities of moral goodness, love, virtue, and righteousness with no possibility of being to the contrary. God is capable of nothing else. It is this fact that sets Him apart from all opposing characteristics and behaviors. That is the quality that makes God so different from what we encounter in the physical world. We are used to dealing with flawed individuals who are capable of exhibiting both positive and negative behaviors:

- good one minute and evil the next
- telling the truth now and lying later
- malicious today and loving tomorrow as the mood changes

God can do no such thing. He is unchanging (Heb. 13:8; John 14:9). God always tells the truth, and it is impossible for Him to lie. God always is good, and it is impossible for Him to be evil. This is what it means for God to be benevolent and one-sided. It is impossible for Him to be malevolent. God is set apart from all such things, and that is what makes God holy and pure. Perhaps another way of expressing it is to say God is always true to Himself. He is consistent for He can never be anything else.

As we consider the concept of holiness and how it applies to the revealed nature of God, sometimes a question arises. Why didn't God create humankind to be holy and good, just like God, endowed with that same benevolent nature of wholesomeness and purity? The answer is, He did. By God's original design and plan, He made humankind in His image/likeness. That included giving humankind an eternal spirit and endowing that spirit with a holiness patterned after the nature of God Himself. This is exactly what took place in the creation of Adam and Eve as described in Genesis 1:26–27. During this initial period, Adam and Eve lived in a perfectly harmonious relationship with God, enjoying full fellowship with their Creator.

As an aside, it is worth noting that despite all that has taken place since the creation of Adam and Eve, it always has been God's desire for humankind to choose to be holy and live a pure and wholesome life. God spoke through Moses to the nation of Israel by saying, "You shall be Holy, for I the Lord your God am Holy" (Lev. 19:2).

In the New Testament teachings, the apostle Peter commanded the same thing by citing Old Testament scripture: "But like the Holy One who called you, be holy yourselves also in all your behavior; because it is written, 'You shall be Holy, for I am Holy'" (1 Pet. 1:15–16). So, if Adam and Eve were created holy and God commanded humankind to be holy just as God is holy, then what went wrong? What changed? The answer is sin.

What is sin? The word *sin* is used a lot in religious communities. It is found in the English translations of the Bible in the Old and New Testaments. People generally associate sin with conduct that is bad or evil in the sight of God. These are things that God does not want us to do, and this is all true. However, there is a much more enlightened understanding available to us by looking at the Hebrew and Greek Bible manuscripts. There we can examine the meaning of the inspired words that are translated as *sin* in our English versions of the Bible. Interestingly enough, in the original languages the meaning of these words is "to miss the mark." When we read about people sinning, God literally is telling us they were missing the mark. Having said that, how do we relate the idea of missing the mark to our concept and understanding of what it means to sin? If sinning is missing the mark, then what is the mark we are missing? Based on God's original design and intent for humankind, that mark can be identified as the holy nature of God.

In the beginning, when Adam and Eve were created in the image and likeness of God, they shared all the qualities of His nature. They were holy and pure because God created them that way. Adam and Eve had no awareness of missing the mark because they were completely in step with their Creator following after His will. However, it was never God's intent to create a family of robots forced to be holy like Him. Instead, God provided humankind with the intelligence and free will to make individual choices. God wanted us to love Him enough to choose to remain holy and pure and thereby be like Him.

Adam and Eve were given a choice based on the trees in the Garden of Eden. God commanded them to eat freely from any tree in the garden except from the Tree of the Knowledge of Good and Evil (Gen. 2:16–17). They were forbidden to eat from that single tree under the penalty of death. When Adam and Eve ate from the Tree of the Knowledge of Good and Evil, they missed the mark and sinned. At that point, their eyes were opened, and they became aware of the alluring distinction between good and evil. For us today, God's desire is unchanged. He still wants us to be holy as He is holy (1 Pet. 1:15–16) and through the teachings found in the Bible, God has revealed what it takes to be holy and conform to His image and likeness.

The Bible provides us with warnings about the different ways we can fall into sin and thereby miss the mark. Perhaps the most common way is to break God's law and violate His direct commandments and teachings. In other words, disobeying a commandment of God in an act of lawlessness (1 John 3:4). This includes things like stealing when God has taught us not to steal or taking a life by committing murder when God says to love one another. These are rebellious acts defying God's will for us.

Another way we can sin is to go too far by going beyond the teachings of Christ (2 John 9). When we willfully act outside the bounds of God's nature by following our own selfish desires, we no longer have God. We have abandoned Him to go our own way. This is reminiscent of Proverbs 16:25: "There is a way which seems right to a man, but its end is the way of death." What seems right to us may not be right before God. This is because our thoughts are not God's thoughts—and our ways are not God's ways (Isa. 55:8).

A third example of sinning is when we do not do what we should (James 4:17). This is sometimes called a passive sin or sin by inaction. Adhering to the nature of God does not just mean avoiding actions contrary to God's will. Adhering to the nature of God also means doing what God expects us to do. In the example of James chapter 4, it means including God and spiritual considerations in our life choices and decision-making process. This requires us to have a conscious awareness of our spiritual obligations to God and to each other.

Finally, there is another important reality of sin as it applies to all humankind. It is the fact that "all have sinned and fall short of the glory of God" (Rom. 3:23). The scriptures reveal that—with the exception of Jesus Christ—everyone who has ever lived to an age of accountability has missed the mark and sinned. None of us has ever lived a perfectly holy life. This reality now positions us to address the questions we started with: Why should I care about spiritual things? More specifically, so what if I have sinned? The answers reside in something called the problem of sin.

First of all, note that even in the physical realm, sin leads to consequences and hardships directly attributed to unholy conduct that misses the mark of God. For example, when we break God's law and steal, we can be arrested and sent to jail. If we commit murder, we might spend our remaining lifetime in prison or be executed for the crime. By lying, we can destroy a friendship or be fired for falsifying a job application. Fornication and adultery are responsible for emotional distress, broken families, divorce, unexpected pregnancies, and sexually transmitted diseases. Drugs and alcohol can lead to addictions, financial ruin, and serious health problems. None of these are desirable outcomes. All are physical problems directly attributed to sin, and many can lead to life-changing harm, permanent disability, or premature death. As bad as these things are, there is something much worse. Sin also has consequences in the spiritual realm. In Romans 6:23, the apostle Paul says, "The wages of sin is death." The death that Paul is speaking about is not physical death. Rather, it is a spiritual death that is here contrasted with the alternative: the gift of eternal life. The greatest problem of sin is that it kills us spiritually.

To appreciate the significance of spiritual death, we must examine how and why sin affects our relationships to God. In the beginning, when Adam and Eve were created in the image and likeness of God, they were holy and pure just as God is. In that state, there was a special relationship and bond between humankind and God. Adam and Eve existed in full fellowship with their Creator. They were spiritually one with God and in total conformity with His nature. This provided them with free access to their Creator as well as all the blessings that came from that relationship. When they sinned by eating the forbidden fruit, that perfect bond was broken. They were alienated from God. This is what God had warned them would happen when He said, "In the day you eat from it you shall surely die" (Gen. 2:17).

The same thing happens to us when, by our own choosing, we sin and miss the mark. Our spiritual relationship and fellowship with God is severed. Sin produces a barrier between us and God (as illustrated in Figure 2).

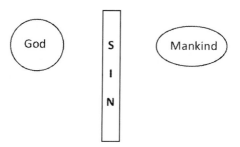

Figure 2. Our sin produces a barrier separating us from God.

This is what is meant by the spiritual death and wages of sin referenced by the apostle Paul in Romans 6:23. It also is described by Isaiah the prophet.

> Behold, the Lord's hand is not so short that it cannot save; Nor is His ear so dull that it cannot hear. But your iniquities have made a separation between you and your God, and your sins have hidden His face from you so that He does not hear. (Isa. 59:1–2)

This separation is not just a matter of God's own choosing. Rather, it is a necessity resulting from the holy nature of God. First of all, note that God cannot simply ignore our sins. Were God to ignore our disobedience (lawbreaking), He would no longer be just and righteous. That would be an unjust and unrighteous response contrary to His nature. Justice demands there be a consequence for sin. Secondly, the consequence for sin is not arbitrary. It must result in a separation from God because a holy God cannot continue in fellowship with sinners. Were God to do so, He would no longer be "set apart" or holy. One might say our sin would taint Him. These things can never happen because by definition God is pure, always true to Himself and His nature. God is now and forever holy, set apart from sin.

There is still the question as to whether being separated from God is really all that bad. When we look around us today, we see a world filled with both good and evil. Good people often are abused and suffer while trying to uphold godly values. In contrast, many who practice evil thrive in pleasure, power, fame, and riches. It might seem as though there is no great advantage in following after a holy God. To put this in proper perspective, however, we must take into account the unique and temporary circumstances active here in the physical world.

In James 1:17, the Bible says, "Every good thing bestowed and every perfect gift is from above, coming down from the Father of lights, with whom there is no variation, or shifting shadow." All the good things experienced in this world are provided to us by God. He is responsible for everything we need to sustain our physical existence, and His spiritual nature is seen in the elements of holiness visible among those who strive to conform to His will.

God is responsible for all the godly blessings of happiness, peace, joy, goodness, love, comfort, light, and hope that exist in the world today. So, if God is responsible for all the good in the world, where does all the evil come from—and why does God allow it? Once again, the answer is sin. All evil in the world today arises from the consequences of sin. God allows it for now because He granted us free will with the ability to choose for ourselves how we will behave. Unfortunately, we often choose poorly. Our sins lead to bad outcomes for us, and they can affect the lives of countless innocent others. Adultery and fornication can harm marriages, spouses, and children. Violence and crime can destroy property and the lives of entire families. Greed, pride, and lust cause senseless pain in our society.

To add to this mix, we are told there is a spirit actively opposing God and stirring up trouble in the world today. The devil— through the serpent—first deceived Eve into eating the forbidden fruit (Gen. 3:1–7). For that reason, he is called the serpent of old (Rev. 12:9) and the father of lies (John 8:44). The apostle Peter describes the devil as prowling about like a roaring lion seeking someone to devour by leading them to sin (1 Pet. 5:8).

In the physical realm of God's creation, good and evil are allowed to exist together. God "causes His sun to rise on the evil and the good, and sends rain on the righteous and the unrighteous" (Matt. 5:45). From this passage, Jesus makes it clear that God's earthly blessings extend to all humankind. Both the good and the evil people in the world are given the full benefit of all God has provided. A graphic depiction of the two spirits and some of what they contribute to our earthly environment is shown in Figure 3.

Figure 3. During our time on earth, we live in a world with sin and its consequences, but God's blessings freely flow to all.

43

At first glance, this may not seem fair. However, we must not overlook the fact that God created humankind to be special, possessing not only a body of flesh and blood but an eternal spirit. While it is true sinners may live and prosper for eighty, ninety, or one hundred years, the body eventually withers, dies, and returns to the dust of the ground (Gen. 3:19). The spirit, however, is eternal, and when the physical body dies, that spirit lives on and returns to God who gave it (Eccl. 12:7). Therein lies the issue. What happens when our physical existence ends and our fleshly body dies?

The apostle Paul taught us there will be a day when Jesus returns, dealing out retribution to those who are separated from God by sin. In 2 Thessalonians 1:9, the Bible says, "These will pay the penalty of eternal destruction, away from the presence of the Lord and from the glory of His power." There are two important points to be made here. First, the ultimate consequences of sin are realized in the spiritual realm and not in the physical realm. These consequences are eternal, meaning they endure beyond all physical things when time itself is no more. This is the final (end) state that will never change. Second, this state of destruction is known as *spiritual death*. It involves a total separation from God in eternity. God's presence and influence are removed with no hope of ever being restored. Since God alone provides every good thing and perfect gift (James 1:17), being separated from God also means being separated from every godly blessing. This is equivalent to an existence without anything God supplies. That means all happiness, peace, joy, goodness, love, comfort, light, and hope will disappear forever. That leaves only an ungodly environment with sorrow, conflict, weeping, evil, hate, torment, darkness, and hopelessness. This is a state of unimaginable anguish with no prospect for relief. The Bible calls this state *hell*. Figure 4 illustrates the significance of an eternal separation from God.

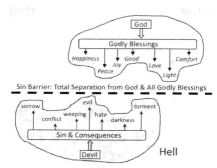

*Figure 4. Hell is an eternal separation from God
and from all the blessings He supplies.*

Hell is not some contrived torture chamber designed by God to inflict pain and punishment on humankind. It is a lost state resulting from the total absence of God. Furthermore, this lost condition is not the result of God leaving us. It is caused by our choosing to depart from Him and His holy ways. This is the one and only occasion when humankind will be subjected to an environment totally without God. Since we have always lived in a world with God present, we have never experienced a state of such despair. To help us grasp the severity of this condition, the Bible describes hell using vivid physical terms we are more likely to comprehend so as to paint a picture of a place we would want to avoid at all costs. Hell is described as a place of eternal fire (Matt. 25:41) and outer darkness with weeping and gnashing of teeth (Matt. 8:12).

Although those living in sin will be subject to eternal destruction when Jesus returns, those who die before then will experience it immediately. In Luke 16:19–31, there is an account of the deaths of a rich man and a poor man named Lazarus. After death, the rich sinner was separated from God immediately. He was in a place of agony and torment, burning and pleading for mercy. It is clear from these verses that all will face the consequences of sin when they reach the spiritual realm—in death or when Christ makes His next appearance.

In chapter 4, we have learned why we should care about spiritual things. Since all have sinned and fall short of the glory of God (Rom. 3:23), the outlook for all humankind appears hopeless. As sinners, we face an eternal separation from God in the anguish of hell. Romans 6:23, however, tells us there is an alternative to spiritual death: the gift of eternal life. If our sins can be blotted out and Holiness restored, then the sin barrier separating us from God is removed. Without sin, our fellowship with God resumes, and we can look forward to an eternity with Him.

Being in the presence of God means experiencing all the blessing God supplies. This will be a holy environment totally without evil since sin and all its consequences will have been removed permanently. The Bible calls this state heaven.

> And I saw the holy city, new Jerusalem, coming down out of heaven from God, made ready as a bride adorned for her husband. And I heard a loud voice from the throne, saying, "Behold, the tabernacle of God is among men, and He will dwell among them, and they shall be His people, and God Himself will be among them, and He will wipe away every tear from their eyes; and there will no longer be any death; there will no longer be any mourning, or crying, or pain; the first things have passed away." (Rev. 21:2–4)

It is clear that sin is what makes the difference between an eternity in heaven and an eternity in hell (as shown in Figure 5).

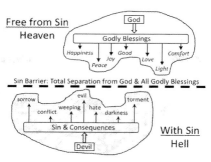

Figure 5. *Sin is what causes us to be separated from God in hell; without sin, our fellowship with God secures a future in heaven.*

Fortunately for us, God is a benevolent God of love. God wants to save us from the terrible outcome of hell. He has no desire for us to be lost in eternity. In God's eyes, we are all precious and special. After all, we were created that way being given an eternal spirit and made in His image and likeness. The question is, how can a holy God restore us to fellowship with Him without violating His nature and holiness? That is the subject of chapter 5.

CHAPTER 5
God's Solution to the Problem of Sin

Humankind has chased the dream of immortality throughout the ages, being drawn by an unquenchable appetite for the pleasures of life. Typically, that dream focuses on fleshly desires, fame, fortune, and success, while somehow managing to overlook the worldly pain and sorrow naturally arising from the consequences of sin. The irony is immortality already has been achieved—not physically but on God's terms in the spiritual realm. God granted it to us when He created humankind in His own image and likeness. Our physical bodies were equipped with a spirit that survives physical death and will live on in eternity. The question is, will that existence be with or without God? Left on our own, we chase after the things of the world:

- the lust of the flesh
- the lust of the eyes
- the boastful pride of life (1 John 2:16)

As we give in to temptations, we sin against God by missing the targeted holy behavior that He has desired from us since the beginning. When that happens, our spiritual bond with God is broken because a holy God cannot maintain fellowship with sinners (Figure 2). The problem of sin is that it leads to a spiritual separation that extends beyond the physical realm into eternity (Isa. 59:1–2; Matt. 25:41).

With an eternal separation from God comes a separation from all the blessings God supplies. Without them, we are left in an ungodly, unholy environment that the Bible describes as a place of darkness, torment, and hopelessness (Matt. 8:12; 25:41). That is the reality of hell and spiritual death. The disaster comes from the fact that all of us have sinned (Rom. 3:23). Without some form of intervention, our destiny is an eternity separated from God in hell. By now, any reasonable person would be in a state of near panic, asking, "Is there a solution to the problem of sin?" That is the subject of chapter 5.

One might begin by considering whether there is something we can do to save ourselves. For example, could we simply throw ourselves on the mercy of God and ask for His unconditional forgiveness? Although that may sound well, since God is known to be loving and merciful, it alone does not work (at least not without some other factors to be considered shortly). The problem with this approach comes from the fact that God is just and righteous. Sin or lawbreaking must be accompanied by consequences to maintain God's state of righteousness and to be true to the just nature of God. If God simply ignored our behavior or granted unconditional forgiveness, justice would not be served—and God would not be set apart from sin. This would make God unjust and unrighteous and violate His holy nature. Since that can never happen, this scheme will not save us.

As another possibility, suppose we were to perform good works to try to make up for sinful disobedience. While it may seem reasonable, this is unacceptable even in a secular judicial system. Good deeds do not reverse the consequences of breaking the law. All the good done by a murderer will not bring a dead victim back to life. Our legal system has no statute of limitations for killing someone. In our society, despite years of godly living, a murderer still must go to trial, even years later, to face the justice of the court. Moreover, in Ephesians 2:8–9, the apostle Paul clearly teaches that humankind is not saved as a result of works so that no one may boast. We cannot earn salvation. Once we have broken God's law, we are lawbreakers. Good works do not change that fact. We are still guilty before the court of God.

Alternatively, could we just find someone else to take the blame for our sin? Blaming others for our shortcomings seems to be a skill most of us have mastered. Perhaps there is a loved one who is willing to fall before God and say, "Punish me for the sin of another." In that case, there is a sacrificial offering and a consequence proposed for my sin. Although this seems appealing, it neglects the fact that "all have sinned and fall short of the glory of God" (Rom. 3:23). What that means is any accountable person willing to take my sin is already guilty of sin and deserving spiritual death for his or her own actions. Hence, such an offering is worthless and meaningless. Sinners cannot offer themselves for the life of another because they are already spiritually dead from their own sin. A just sacrifice would require someone who lived a perfect, holy life to willingly accept the burden and consequences of the sins from another.

At this point, it should be clear. By our own means, there is nothing humankind can do to make up for past sins. If there is to be a solution to the problem of sin, that solution must come from God. What could it be? How can a holy God save us without violating His nature and still remain set apart from sin? Perhaps an even better question is, why would God want to do so?

Fortunately for us, God is not only holy and just; He is also a God of Love. First John 4:8 states, "The one who does not love does not know God, for God is love." God's love for humankind is rooted in the fact that, among all the creation, only humankind was created in His image and likeness. It is our dual nature that makes us so unique, having a living physical form of flesh and blood and an eternal spirit that will survive our mortal bodies.

We are special and share a common spiritual bond with the

Creator. Ultimately, this explains the great lengths to which God was willing to go to preserve the relationship and fellowship with humankind. Love, however, does not allow God to abandon His holy nature and unconditionally pardon sinners. Holiness still requires God to be set apart from sin, while righteousness and justice also are preserved. So, how is God able to reconnect with us bridging the spiritual gap created by sin? This required the ultimate sacrifice, one that only God could provide—an offering of the Son of God as a living sacrifice. "By this the love of God was manifested in us, that God has sent His only begotten Son into the world so that we might live through Him" (1 John 4:9).

The idea of a living sacrifice for the forgiveness of sins was part of the Old Covenant, but these offerings were from animals. Under the Law of Moses, given to the nation of Israel, God commanded His chosen people to make a sin offering on the Day of Atonement. As part of this cleansing, bulls and goats were slaughtered before the altar. God required the shedding of blood for the atonement of sin.

> For the life of the flesh is in the blood, and I have given it to you on the altar to make atonement for your souls; for it is the blood by reason of the life that makes atonement. (Lev. 17:11)

By requiring a blood sacrifice for atonement, God made clear the association between sin and death. The cost for sin involved a loss of life. Although God granted forgiveness to the nation of Israel on the Day of Atonement, the people were not justified by the blood of bulls and goats. "For it is impossible for the blood of bulls and goats to take away sins" (Heb. 10:4). Animals are but flesh and blood without a spirit. They, in and of themselves, have nothing to offer God as a sin sacrifice.

Sacrifices under the Law of Moses were only a shadow of the good things to come (Heb. 10:1). In those sacrifices, there was a reminder of sins year by year (Heb. 10:3), but the cleansing and atonement was attained through the New Covenant established by the death of Jesus Christ (to be discussed shortly).

> For this reason He is the mediator of a new covenant, so that, since a death has taken place for the redemption of the transgressions that were committed under the first covenant, those who have been called may receive the promise of the eternal inheritance. For where a covenant is, there must of necessity be the death of the one who made it. (Heb. 9:15–16)

"By this will we have been sanctified through the offering of the body of Jesus Christ once for all" (Heb. 10:10). Forgiveness of sins is attainable only through the sacrifice of Jesus. The apostle Peter put it this way: "And there is salvation in no one else; for there is no other name under heaven that has been given among men by which we must be saved" (Acts 4:12).

Who was this Jesus—and why was He so special? In his letter to the Philippians, the apostle Paul wrote:

> Have this attitude in yourselves which was also in Christ Jesus, who, although He existed in the form of God, did not regard equality with God a thing to be grasped, but emptied Himself, taking the form of a bond-servant, and being made in the likeness of men. Being found in appearance as a man, He humbled Himself by becoming obedient to the point of death, even death on a cross. For this reason also, God highly exalted Him, and bestowed on Him the name which is above every name, so that at the name of Jesus every knee will bow, of those who are in heaven and on earth

and under the earth, and that every tongue will confess that Jesus Christ is Lord, to the glory of God the Father. (Phil. 2:5–11)

Further evidence for the identity of Jesus was provided to Peter, James, and John when Jesus was transfigured in glory before them, shining intensely as the voice of God, the Father, came from a bright cloud, saying, "This is My beloved Son, with whom I am well-pleased; listen to Him" (Matt. 17:5). These passages reveal the extraordinary nature of Jesus. A human baby was conceived miraculously and born possessing a spirit who was the Son of God. The explanation was given to Joseph in a dream by an angel: "Joseph, son of David, do not be afraid to take Mary as your wife; for the Child who has been conceived in her is of the Holy Spirit. She will bear a Son; and you shall call His name Jesus, for He will save His people from their sins" (Matt. 1:20–21). Through Jesus, the Son of God, deity lived among us as flesh and blood.

Now we can begin to appreciate how God went about providing a solution to the problem of sin. Jesus was able to offer Himself as a unique sacrifice taking our place in a way that none other could. Remember, sinners cannot offer themselves for the salvation of another because they are already spiritually dead from their own sin. An acceptable offering would require someone holy, guiltless, and innocent. Since we are all sinners (Rom. 3:23), we cannot save ourselves or others. However, Jesus as the Son of God was able to live a holy life, free from sin. Hebrews 4:15 states: "For we do not have a high priest who cannot sympathize with our weaknesses, but One who has been tempted in all things as we are, yet without sin."

By living a perfect life, Jesus became eligible to save us from our sins, and He showed us what holy living looks like: "For you have been called for this purpose, since Christ also suffered for you, leaving you an example for you to follow in His steps, who committed no sin, nor was any deceit found in His mouth" (1 Pet. 2:21–22).

Being holy, Jesus offered to substitute Himself as a sin sacrifice in our place, bearing the price for our sins to provide a way for us to be reunited with God. First Peter 3:18 describes this: "For Christ also died for sins once for all, the just for the unjust, so that He might bring us to God, having been put to death in the flesh, but made alive in the spirit."

The apostle Paul confirmed the same in Romans 5:8, "But God demonstrates His own love for us, in that while we were yet sinners, Christ died for us." This was part of a predetermined plan of God.

> Men of Israel, listen to these words: Jesus the Nazarene, a man attested to you by God with miracles and wonders and signs which God performed through Him in your midst, just as you yourselves know—this Man, delivered over by the predetermined plan and foreknowledge of God, you nailed to a cross by the hands of godless men and put Him to death. (Acts 2:22–23)

> In Him we have redemption through His blood, the forgiveness of our trespasses, according to the riches of His grace which He lavished on us. In all wisdom and insight He made known to us the mystery of His will, according to His kind intention which He purposed in Him with a view to an administration suitable to the fullness of the times, that is, the summing up of all things in Christ, things in the heavens and things on the earth. (Eph. 1:7–10)

Jesus willingly laid down His life for the sins of humankind.

> For this reason the Father loves Me, because I lay down My life so that I may take it again. No one has taken it away from Me, but I lay it down on My own initiative. (John 10:17–18)

55

Jesus paid the penalty for our sins in His death on the cross.

> He Himself bore our sins in His body on the cross, so that we might die to sin and live to righteousness; for by His wounds you were healed. For you were continually straying like sheep, but now you have returned to the Shepherd and Guardian of your souls. (1 Pet. 2:24–25)

From this passage, we learn the sins of humankind were placed on Jesus as He hung on the cross. During that time, He suffered for us (1 Pet. 2:21), and yet, by His wounds we were healed to be able to live in righteousness and have a path to reconciliation with God (1 Pet. 2:24).

In an even more descriptive depiction of what was taking place, the Bible says God literally made Jesus become sin for us: "He made Him who knew no sin to be sin on our behalf, so that we might become the righteousness of God in Him" (2 Cor. 5:21). As that happened, God, the Father, had to withdraw from His Son because His holy nature would not allow Him to have fellowship with sin. In the midst of all this, Jesus the man, cried out in agony: "Eloi, Eloi, Lama Sabachthani?" (My God, My God, why have you forsaken Me?)" (Mark 15:34).

For the first time in His existence, Jesus was separated from God, the Father, in spiritual death as He carried the sins of humankind in His body on the cross. Shortly after that "Jesus uttered a loud cry, and breathed His last," experiencing a gruesome physical death from the ordeal of crucifixion (Mark 15:37).

However, the story does not end in the death of Jesus. Jesus rose from the dead just as He had prophesied to His disciples: "The Son of Man is to be delivered into the hands of men, and they will kill Him; and when He has been killed, He will rise three days later" (Mark 9:31). He "was declared the Son of God with power by the resurrection from the dead, according to the Spirit of holiness, Jesus Christ our Lord" (Rom. 1:4).

It is through His resurrection that we have proof and assurance in God's promises that our existence does not end with physical death. The apostle Paul put it this way: "For if we have become united with Him in the likeness of His death, certainly we shall also be in the likeness of His resurrection" (Rom. 6:5). "But now Christ has been raised from the dead, the first fruits of those who are asleep. For since by a man came death, by a man also came the resurrection of the dead. For as in Adam all die, so also in Christ all will be made alive" (1 Cor. 15:20–22).

What took place in Jesus on the cross is a profound demonstration of the love God has for each one of us. Indeed, you are special! Through the humility and willingness of the Son of God to take on human form and allow Himself to be sacrificed on the cross as a price for our sin, we have an opportunity to escape an eternity separated from God in hell. The just and innocent One died in place of the unjust sinner in a sacrifice offered once for all humankind for all time. "For Christ also died for sins once for all, the just for the unjust, so that He might bring us to God, having been put to death in the flesh, but made alive in the spirit" (1 Pet. 3:18). "So Christ also, having been offered once to bear the sins of many, will appear a second time for salvation without reference to sin, to those who eagerly await Him" (Heb. 9:28).

Our path to redemption was secured by the precious blood of Jesus who was sacrificed to save us from our futile way of life.

> If you address as Father the One who impartially judges according to each one's work, conduct yourselves in fear during the time of your stay on earth; knowing that you were not redeemed with perishable things like silver or gold from your futile way of life inherited from your forefathers, but with precious blood, as of a lamb unblemished and spotless, the blood of Christ. (1 Pet. 1:17–19)

"For this is My blood of the covenant, which is poured out for many for forgiveness of sins" (Matt. 26:28). Jesus was the atoning sacrifice who justified us, allowing God a way to pass over our sins.

> Being justified as a gift by His grace through the redemption which is in Christ Jesus; whom God displayed publicly as a propitiation in His blood through faith. This was to demonstrate His righteousness, because in the forbearance of God He passed over the sins previously committed; for the demonstration, I say, of His righteousness at the present time, so that He would be just and the justifier of the one who has faith in Jesus. (Rom. 3:24–26)

Second Corinthians 5:18–19 states, "Now all these things are from God, who reconciled us to Himself through Christ and gave us the ministry of reconciliation, namely, that God was in Christ reconciling the world to Himself, not counting their trespasses against them, and He has committed to us the word of reconciliation." By His willing sacrifice on the cross, Jesus provided the one and only way to restore fellowship between God and humankind (as illustrated in Figure 6).

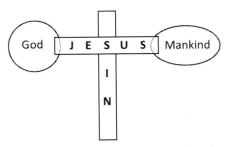

Figure 6. The sacrifice of Jesus on the cross is able to break through the barrier of sin and restore fellowship between God and humankind.

Devising and executing such a plan to offer humankind a path to redemption is simply beyond our ability to comprehend; yet, God's solution to the problem of sin exists through Jesus and is available to us all. What we have not defined is how we go about substituting the sacrifice of Jesus as the payment for our sins. As shown earlier, there is certainly nothing we can do to earn salvation. Redemption is a gift from God, but we still must claim it. We must express our desire to God to be redeemed by the sacrifice of Jesus so we can be made holy in His sight.

God does not grant forgiveness and redemption unconditionally to all humankind whether people want it or not. To do so would be the same as ignoring our sins. Unconditional forgiveness and redemption would allow humankind to live an ungodly, unholy, sinful life of rebellion and maintain fellowship with God in eternity. That would be contrary to God's holy nature, for God is just, righteous, and always must remain separated from sin.

So, how do we claim Jesus as the sacrifice for our sins? What are God's expectations for us? In today's world, among all those who profess to be followers of Jesus Christ, there are disagreements about how we go about laying claim to the sacrifice of Jesus for our redemption and forgiveness of sins. There are generally three different teachings about the steps to salvation:

1. You must first be baptized—then you are saved—and later you are taught and believe.
2. You must first be taught—then believe—after which you are saved—and later baptized.
3. You must first be taught—then believe—after which you are baptized—and then you are saved.

Even though this summary uses some words and concepts that have not yet been defined properly, it is clear these three teachings are entirely different and indeed inconsistent. All of them cannot be true. Key points of distinction revolve around determining what conditions are necessary and sufficient for salvation and when salvation is granted by the forgiveness of sins.

Having differences in the teachings about how to be saved is most troubling since this is a matter of life and death, being saved or being lost, heaven or hell. This is one thing we certainly want to get right. Ultimately, the only way to determine the truth is by studying carefully what God has revealed to us through His written Word. Chapter 6 examines what Jesus taught about God's plan of salvation.

CHAPTER 6

The Path to Salvation Revealed by Jesus

The path to salvation was created when Jesus willingly went to the cross, sacrificing Himself on our behalf to satisfy the justice of a holy God. As a result, there is a way to restore our relationship with God through Jesus as our Redeemer. Paul said, "But God demonstrates His own love toward us, in that while we were yet sinners, Christ died for us. Much more then, having now been justified by His blood, we shall be saved from the wrath of God through Him" (Rom. 5:8–9). Since it is now possible for us to be saved from the wrath of God through Jesus, all that remains is to know how. That is the subject of chapter 6. What did Jesus reveal about the path to salvation?

As we begin examining God's plan of salvation, we want to focus directly on what God says about the subject. We are not interested in the uninspired teachings of men or the traditions of established religious organizations. Since God is the source of all spiritual authority, His words are the only ones that matter. Those words and His message to us come directly through what is revealed in the Bible. "But know this first of all, that no prophecy of scripture is a matter of one's own interpretation, for no prophecy was ever made by an act of human will, but men moved by the Holy Spirit spoke from God" (2 Pet. 1:20–21).

Paul gave a reminder in 2 Timothy 3:16–17: "All Scripture is inspired by God and profitable for teaching, for reproof, for correction, for training in righteousness; so that the man of God may be adequate, equipped for every good work." The teachings about God's plan of salvation are found in the scriptures of the New Testament as part of the Christian Age. We can only discover the truth about salvation by carefully studying the Bible. As always, that is our approach.

To obtain the truth accurately, Bible studies always must be based on sound learning principles. First, we must respect the context of each verse, understanding the setting and intent of the writing. This is necessary to determine what passages apply to us and how we are to use them. Second, we must remember all scripture is inspired and true since it comes to us from a single source—that being God Himself (2 Tim. 3:16–17).

Because all scripture is inspired by God, everything it says is consistent and true. Verses from different chapters or books will never contradict each other. If we detect a conflict among different scriptures, there is something wrong with our understanding of what the Bible teaches. In that case, we must continue studying to find the correct interpretation—one that makes all passages fit together perfectly. The best commentary on a Bible verse comes from other scriptures. By faithfully adhering to these principles, you can "be diligent to present yourself approved to God as a workman who does not need to be ashamed, accurately handling the word of truth" (2 Tim. 2:15).

Because the topic of salvation is so critically important to humankind, God has gone to great lengths to communicate clearly how we go about claiming the sacrifice of Jesus as the payment for our sins. Although the Bible reveals only one path to salvation, that path can be discovered by examining the scriptures in three different ways. Since each way must lead to the same conclusion, this redundancy provides an important check on the accuracy of our understanding.

What are these three study approaches leading us to the plan of salvation?

1. By studying the teachings of Jesus directly. We examine what He—as the author of our salvation—had to say about being saved.
2. By looking at the final instructions Jesus gave to His apostles just before ascending into heaven. We expect these parting words to be among His most important thoughts and commands.
3. By reviewing what the apostles and inspired preachers actually taught and did to bring salvation to a lost world.

If performed properly, all three of these study approaches must take us to the same answer. By carefully pulling all this information together, we can confidently construct a clear picture of what God requires for our redemption and salvation.

We shall begin by examining the teachings of Jesus to learn what He said was necessary for our salvation. Jesus acknowledged the importance of His earthly mission during an encounter with Zaccheus: "For the Son of Man has come to seek and to save that which was lost" (Luke 19:10).

Since Jesus was well aware of what He was to accomplish, it seems only logical to expect that He would spend time talking about salvation during His preaching and teaching ministry, and that He did. Jesus identified four specific things that are "necessary" for salvation, meaning these things must take place if we are to be saved from our sins.

The first salvation requirement Jesus put forth is found in John 8:24 when Jesus spoke to the Jews: "Therefore I said to you that you will die in your sins; for unless you believe that I am He, you will die in your sins." In making this bold statement, Jesus defined something that was absolutely essential to obtain God's forgiveness of sins.

Jesus linked salvation directly to the belief that "I am He." Without that belief, Jesus said, "You will die in your sins," and hence be lost, separated from God for eternity. What did Jesus mean by saying you must believe I am He? Several earlier verses gave the explanation. Jesus said, "I am the bread that came down out of heaven" (John 6:41).

In John 8:12, Jesus said, "I am the light of the world." In verse 18, He said, "I am He who testifies about Myself, and the Father who sent Me testifies about Me." John 8:19 states, "So they were saying to Him, 'Where is Your Father?' Jesus answered, 'You know neither Me, nor My Father; if you knew Me, you would know My Father also.'"

Within these passages, there is a clear reference to Jesus as deity. He called Himself bread that came down from heaven, the light of the world, and one who can bear witness of Himself. He also claimed God as His Father who sent Him. That makes Him the Son of God, a fact taught in scriptures such as Philippians 2:5–11, Luke 1:35, Luke 22:66–70, and John 11:4 to name just a few.

Believing that Jesus is the Son of God is critically important to our salvation. It is the very thing that gives us the way out of the problem of sin. There are, after all, only two possibilities: either Jesus is or He is not the Son of God. If Jesus is not the Son of God, then He is just a man. Even worse—He is a liar. If He is just a man, Jesus would be a sinner like all the rest (Rom. 3:23), and a sinner cannot offer Himself as a sacrifice for the sins of another because sinners must answer for their own guilt.

On the other hand, if Jesus is the Son of God, then He alone is capable of living a perfect, sinless life and sacrificing Himself on behalf of our sins. Without that perfect, sinless sacrifice, there is no solution to the problem of sin, and we are all hopelessly lost. By believing in the deity of Jesus as God living in human form, we accept the truth of all He said and did to offer salvation to humankind:

> Now I make known to you, brethren, the gospel
> which I preached to you, which also you received,
> in which also you stand, by which also you are

saved, if you hold fast the word which I preached
to you, unless you believed in vain. For I delivered
to you as of first importance what I also received,
that Christ died for our sins according to the
Scriptures, and that He was buried, and that
He was raised on the third day according to the
Scriptures. (1 Cor. 15:1–4)

Peter said, "And there is salvation in no one else; for there is no
other name under heaven that has been given among men by which
we must be saved" (Acts 4:12). Our belief in the good news of Jesus
is critical since it is His death, burial, and resurrection that give us
an assured path to salvation with eternal life in heaven. Note the
words of the Hebrew writer: "And without faith it is impossible to
please Him, for he who comes to God must believe that He is and
that He is a rewarder of those who seek Him" (Heb. 11:6).

The second requirement Jesus placed on our salvation involves
repentance. In commenting on the death of those killed by Pilate
while they were offering sacrifices, Jesus admonished his disciples:
"Unless you repent, you will all likewise perish" (Luke 13:3). These
same words were uttered after noting the unexpected calamity of
those trapped under the collapse of the tower of Siloam. There
again, Jesus said, "Unless you repent, you will all likewise perish"
(Luke 13:5).

Repentance also was a key element in the message of John the
Baptist as he prepared the way for the Messiah by fulfilling the
prophecy of Isaiah 40:3. John preached a baptism of repentance
for the forgiveness of sins (Luke 3:3). His message was for all to
"repent, for the kingdom of heaven is at hand" (Matt. 3:2).

As he saw the Pharisees and Sadducees coming for baptism,
John called for them to "bear fruit in keeping with repentance"
(Matt. 3:8). The notion of repentance was echoed by Jesus as He
started His ministry: "Repent, for the kingdom of heaven is at
hand" (Matt. 4:17).

The repentance spoken by John and Jesus refers to a change in heart brought on by godly sorrow (2 Cor. 7:10). It is turning from the pursuit of physical lusts and a life of sin to pursue holiness just as God is holy. That means focusing on godly behavior in an honest attempt to avoid missing the mark. When you think about it, this seems only reasonable. The whole idea of redemption and salvation involves overcoming the barrier between us and God—a barrier that was created by sin.

Our iniquities are what separated us from a holy God in the first place according to Isaiah 59:1–2. That sin is what put us on the path to damnation in hell. If we are determined to remove the sin barrier by appealing to the sacrifice of Jesus to restore our fellowship with God, why would an honest heart want to reconstruct that barrier by continuing in sin?

> For if, after they have escaped the defilements of the world by the knowledge of the Lord and Savior Jesus Christ, they are again entangled in them and are overcome, the last state has become worse for them than the first. For it would be better for them not to have known the way of righteousness, than having known it, to turn away from the holy commandment handed on to them. It has happened to them according to the true proverb, "A dog returns to its own vomit," and "A sow, after washing, returns to wallowing in the mire." (2 Pet. 2:20–22)

There is danger in returning to a life of sin.

> For in the case of those who have once been enlightened and have tasted of the heavenly gift and have been made partakers of the Holy Spirit, and have tasted the good Word of God and the powers of the age to come, and then have fallen

away, it is impossible to renew them again to repentance, since they again crucify to themselves the Son of God and put Him to open shame. For ground that drinks the rain which often falls on it and brings forth vegetation useful to those for whose sake it is also tilled, receives a blessing from God; but if it yields thorns and thistles, it is worthless and close to being cursed, and it ends up being burned. (Heb. 6:4–8)

Paul preached against the idea of continuing to sin while relying on God's grace to cover our willful disobedience: "Are we to continue in sin so that grace may increase? May it never be! How shall we who died to sin still live in it?" (Rom. 6:1–2). Paul also preached about the importance of repentance.

Even so consider yourselves to be dead to sin, but alive to God in Christ Jesus. Therefore do not let sin reign in your mortal body so that you obey its lusts, and do not go on presenting the members of your body to sin as instruments of unrighteousness; but present yourselves to God as those alive from the dead, and your members as instruments of righteousness to God. (Rom. 6:11–13)

An appeal for forgiveness and salvation must go hand in hand with a change in heart, turning to a holy lifestyle just as God is holy (1 Pet. 1:13–16). Without a desire and commitment to repent, an appeal for forgiveness is insincere and equivalent to asking God to save us but allow us to continue living in sin. That is impossible for a holy God (Isa. 59:1–2).

As a third condition for salvation, Jesus said we must publically confess the name of Jesus. Confession is openly professing our belief in Jesus as the Son of God and author of our salvation. It provides accountability and ownership for our belief as well as an explanation to the world for the changes in heart and behavior that come from godly repentance. Luke 12:8–9 states, "And I say to you, everyone who confesses Me before men, the Son of Man will confess him also before the angels of God; but he who denies Me before men will be denied before the angels of God."

In Matthew 10:32–33, Jesus spoke to His disciples saying: "Therefore everyone who confesses Me before men, I will also confess him before My Father who is in heaven. But whoever denies Me before men, I will also deny him before My Father who is in heaven." By confessing the name of Jesus before humankind, we are assured that Jesus will be our advocate, acknowledging us before the Father in heaven. Alternatively, Jesus tells us if we reject Him before others, He too will deny us before the Father. Paul cited this principle in 2 Timothy 2:11–13: "It is a trustworthy statement: For if we died with Him, we will also live with Him; If we endure, we will also reign with Him; If we deny Him, He also will deny us; If we are faithless, He remains faithful, for He cannot deny Himself."

The fourth and last requirement Jesus placed on our salvation comes from being baptized. This is also part of what is called the Great Commission. In Mark 16:16, Jesus said, "He who has believed and has been baptized shall be saved; but he who has disbelieved shall be condemned."

This scripture makes a contrast between conditions leading to salvation and those leading to condemnation. In the first part of the verse, we learn salvation results from a personal response that begins with belief and ends with baptism. Jesus taught that believers will be saved if they are baptized. In the second part of the verse, He confirmed that without the first step of belief, all are condemned and neither baptism nor anything else matters. This is consistent with the prior teaching in John 8:24 where Jesus made belief a necessary condition for salvation by saying, "Unless you believe that I am He, you will die in your sins."

The biblical definition of baptism comes from an examination of the Greek text in the early New Testament manuscripts as copied from the inspired writers. The meaning of the Greek word is to *immerse, submerge,* or *completely overwhelm.* It does not mean to sprinkle or pour. Although there are words that would translate as *sprinkling* and *pouring,* they are never used by the inspired writers in this context.

Unfortunately, the actual word found in the Greek manuscripts was not translated in any of the common English versions of the New Testament. Instead, a transliteration was performed whereby English letters were substituted for the Greek ones to create a new English word *baptize.* This, of course, was done without justification and obscures the linkage of this made-up English word to the meaning of the original Greek. Unfortunately, this also makes it easier for others to alter the intended meaning to something that better suits their own purpose or doctrine. It does not, however, change the fact that the true meaning of God's inspired Word is *to immerse.*

From the context of many different scriptures, it is clear that the inspired text of the New Testament defines baptism as a total immersion in water. John baptized in water (John 1:26) at Aenon near Salim because John 3:23 says there was much water at that location. John chose that specific site because there was enough water to immerse large crowds of people. This is much more water than would have been required for sprinkling or pouring. Also, John preached a baptism of repentance for the forgiveness of sins, linking baptism directly to salvation. The baptism of the Ethiopian eunuch provides further evidence as to the act being a total immersion in water. The participants had to travel to a location of sufficient water for baptism (Acts 8:36). Once there, they went down into the water (v. 38) and after immersion came up out of the water (v. 39). There is no textual justification or biblical example of baptism being performed by an act of sprinkling or pouring. These are man-made traditions that are not found in the Bible.

Jesus also alluded to the necessity of water baptism in His remarks to Nicodemus recorded in John 3. Prior to this encounter, three important events had taken place:

1. John the Baptist had made his appearance bearing witness of the coming Messiah, and he was performing a water baptism of repentance for the forgiveness of sins (John 1:15; Luke 3:3).
2. John had baptized Jesus and people beheld the Spirit descending upon Jesus as a dove out of heaven (Luke 3:21–22).
3. Jesus had begun His ministry performing signs and wonders to confirm the word while echoing the same message as John for all to "repent for the kingdom of heaven is at hand" (Matt. 4:17).

When Nicodemus approached Jesus that night and began acknowledging Him as a teacher from God, "Jesus answered and said to him, 'Truly, truly, I say to you, unless one is born again he cannot see the kingdom of God'" (John 3:3). Jesus was explaining to Nicodemus what must be done to enter the kingdom of God. He had to be born again. This confused Nicodemus for he was thinking of a physical rebirth. Jesus, however, was talking about a spiritual birth consistent with the message of repentance that was being preached by John and Jesus.

From that confused perspective, Nicodemus asked Jesus how an old man can be born a second time. Jesus answered, "Truly, truly, I say to you, unless one is born of water and the Spirit he cannot enter into the kingdom of God" (John 3:5). Jesus was talking to a man who already had passed through his mother's womb at physical birth, telling him how it was now possible for him to be born again, this time into the kingdom of God. The second birth required two elements: water and the Spirit. Bear in mind, the only familiarity Nicodemus would have had with the concept of being born again through water would have come from the baptism of repentance being practiced by John the Baptist.

Nicodemus also would have been aware that the Spirit descended from heaven as a dove landing upon Jesus after Jesus arose from the water of baptism (Matt. 3:16–17). John himself publically bore witness of that fact in John 1:32–34. So, when Jesus spoke of being born of water and the Spirit, Nicodemus logically would have attributed this to a baptism of repentance, bringing with it a change of heart. That is just as Jesus intended. Jesus also was providing Nicodemus with a preview of the path to salvation that would be imposed during the coming age of Christianity.

Spiritual renewal was the message of John as well as the later teaching by Jesus in Mark 16:16 and by the apostles during their ministry. The purpose and significance of water immersion will be discussed in chapter 9. For now, it is sufficient to note that baptism is immersion in water, and Jesus cited baptism as a necessary condition to enter the kingdom of God and be saved.

In summary, when Jesus says something must be done to obtain salvation, that something becomes a requirement since it is cited as a necessary condition. This does not mean a necessary condition is sufficient for salvation because other conditions also may be required. Since all scripture is inspired and true, if more than one requirement is specified in the Bible, then all requirements must be satisfied to obtain salvation. Otherwise, something Jesus designated as necessary is being left undone/unsatisfied. From the direct teachings of Jesus, we have identified four things that He said were required for salvation:

- belief
- repentance
- confession
- baptism

Since these are the only four requirements Jesus specified, we conclude that these four conditions are both necessary and sufficient for obtaining salvation. In other words, we lay claim to the sacrifice of Jesus as a payment for our sins and are saved from the wrath of God only when we have satisfied all four requirements: believing, repenting, confessing, and being baptized. This is God's plan of salvation for humankind as derived directly from the teaching of Jesus.

As a first check on the accuracy of our understanding of God's plan of salvation, we shall examine the words Jesus spoke to His apostles just before He ascended into heaven. We are looking for consistency. Because these are His parting words, we expect them to contain vital instructions that define His expectations for the ministry of the apostles that would follow. The biblical text is found in three passages commonly called the Great Commission.

In the first account, Jesus said:

> All authority has been given to Me in heaven and on earth. Go therefore and make disciples of all the nations, baptizing them in the name of the Father and the Son and the Holy Spirit, teaching them to observe all that I commanded you; and lo, I am with you always, even to the end of the age. (Matt. 28:18–20)

In this passage, Jesus makes several distinct points. First, He justified His right to issue the subsequent commands by citing His authority over everything in heaven and on earth. In other words, He declared Himself to be the One in charge. Second, He commanded His apostles to go to all nations and make disciples, i.e., grow followers who are dedicated to keeping His Word. Third, Jesus actually defined how to make these disciples. He said to baptize them in the name of the Father, Son, and Holy Spirit and then to teach the baptized followers to observe all that Jesus had commanded. Jesus concluded by offering them the encouragement of knowing they are not alone in this undertaking. He promised to be with them always. In issuing these commands, Jesus was instructing His apostles about how they were to continue the work of salvation after Jesus physically departed from them. Jesus specifically mentioned the importance of baptizing believers to make disciples and continuing to teach them to equip them for Christian living and service.

In another account of the Great Commission, Jesus said,

> Thus it is written, that the Christ would suffer and rise again from the dead the third day, and that repentance for forgiveness of sins would be proclaimed in His name to all the nations, beginning from Jerusalem. (Luke 24:46–47)

Here, Jesus references the prophecy of the gospel and the good news of the death, burial, and resurrection of Jesus, which secured the path to salvation for humankind through His sacrifice. The message that was to be preached first in Jerusalem and spread to all nations included a call to repentance for the purpose of obtaining the forgiveness of sins. This made repentance a necessary condition for salvation.

The third account of the Great Commission was mentioned in the prior section on the teachings of Jesus. Nevertheless, it is repeated here for completeness and comparison.

> And He said to them, "Go into all the world and preach the gospel to all creation. He who has believed and has been baptized shall be saved; but he who has disbelieved shall be condemned." (Mark 16:15–16)

As before, we see Jesus calling for the gospel to be preached to all the world. He promises that those who believe and are baptized shall be saved, meaning their sins shall be forgiven.

These accounts of the Great Commission represent the last instructions of Jesus to His apostles. In them, we see how God planned to offer salvation to the lost world. Although these passages do not record word for word everything that Jesus said, they do represent summaries provided by three inspired writers. That means everything written is true.

To construct the complete picture of what Jesus commanded His apostles to do, we must combine the instructions from all three accounts. When we pull all the information together, we come up with the following composite defining what the apostles were commanded to do:

- Go to all nations to all the world.
- Preach the gospel (good news) of Jesus.
- Make disciples who believe, repent, and are baptized in the name of the Father, Son, and Holy Spirit (those disciples were promised to receive the forgiveness of sins and be saved).
- Teach them to observe all that Jesus had commanded.

These instructions explicitly mention belief, repentance, and baptism. Although a confession that Jesus is the Son of God is not directly specified in these accounts, it is still there implicitly. Disciples are to be baptized in the name of the Father, Son, and Holy Spirit. By being baptized in their names, disciples are placing themselves into the service and ownership of Father, Son, and Holy Spirit. Therefore, submitting to baptism commanded by and in the name of the Son is an acknowledgement and confession of a belief in the authority of Jesus as the Son of God.

In summary, what we see in the Great Commission is Jesus commanding His apostles to bring salvation to a lost world by making disciples who believe, repent, confess (implied), and are baptized to obtain the forgiveness of sins. This is consistent with the teachings Jesus shared during his earthly ministry.

We have yet one more truth check available to us. We can investigate how the apostles and other inspired evangelists interpreted these commands by examining the steps they took to implement the Great Commission. That is reported in chapter 7.

CHAPTER 7
The Plan of Salvation Presented to Humankind

Chapter 6 reviewed the teachings of Jesus to discover what He said we must do to be saved from our sins and restored to fellowship with our heavenly Father. That study uncovered four things that Jesus said were necessary for salvation.

The first step is to believe in Jesus as the Son of God whose death, burial, and resurrection secured our salvation. Only deity in human form is able to live a perfect, sinless life. It is that perfection that allowed Jesus to sacrifice Himself on our behalf, taking the consequence for our sins to satisfy the justice of a holy God. By paying our debt, He was able to create a path for our redemption, giving us an option for a solution to the problem of sin.

As a second condition for salvation, we must repent of our sinful lifestyles. The idea of repentance is to turn away from sinning by changing our hearts to follow after the holiness of God. It encompasses sorrow, regret, and a desire to remove the sin separating us from God and to try our best to avoid sinning again.

Thirdly, Jesus said we must be willing to confess His name before men. This is where we take ownership of the belief in Jesus as the Son of God, our Savior. It is an acknowledgement that we want to be disciples of Jesus and offer this as an explanation for our change in heart and lifestyle.

The fourth thing Jesus mentioned is the need for baptism. From the Greek word in the early manuscripts, we know this to be an immersion in water authorized by Jesus Himself. Believers who had repented and confessed were baptized in the name of Jesus as the last condition necessary for salvation. A further explanation of the significance of baptism is offered in chapter 9.

Jesus specified these same criteria during the Great Commission. He issued final commands to His apostles, telling them how to implement the plan of salvation. That consistency of message gives us confidence that we have correctly identified the steps involved in God's plan of salvation for humankind. In chapter 7, we shall investigate the teachings and actions of the apostles and other inspired preachers as they executed the commands of Jesus. This will serve as a final check, confirming that we accurately have determined what must be done to claim Jesus as the sacrifice for our sins.

The book of Acts contains the early history of the church and a summary of what took place when people were saved by obeying the commands of Jesus. The record of the apostles' ministry begins in Acts 2 where the apostles received miraculous power as the Holy Spirit came upon them during the gathering of the Jews in Jerusalem on the day of Pentecost. This was the fulfillment of the promise Jesus made to send a Helper who would teach them all things, guide them into all truth, and bring to remembrance all that Jesus had taught them (John 14:16, 26; John 16:13).

The apostles had been instructed to go to Jerusalem until they were clothed with power from on high (Luke 24:49). That power was to equip them for the task of being witnesses in Jerusalem, in all Judea, Samaria, and to the remotest parts of the earth (Acts 1:8). On this occasion, the apostles first preached the gospel message (i.e., good news) bringing salvation to the Jews. That preaching was to Jews assembled from many nations since the apostles were able to recount the mighty deeds of God in the different languages of the people through the power bestowed by the Holy Spirit (Acts 2:5–11).

Peter explained this miraculous event as a fulfillment of the prophecy of Joel 2:28–32. Peter continued by describing how Jesus—even though affirmed by many signs and wonders from God—had been put to death on the cross by them, according to the predetermined plan and foreknowledge of God. Even so, God raised Him from the dead, proving His power over death, and then exalted Him to the right hand of God (Acts 2:22–24, 33).

When Peter concluded his remarks by telling them this same Jesus was the Lord and promised Messiah, the Anointed One of Israel whom they had crucified, the people were "pierced to the heart" (Acts 2:37). At that point, they realized they had murdered God's chosen one and were anguishing over what they had done. In a dire sense of panic, they cried out asking: "Brethren," (i.e., countrymen, fellow Jews), "what shall we do?" (Acts 2:37). Foremost on their minds was determining how to obtain forgiveness and get right in the eyes of God. Specifically, they wanted to know what action and what steps they should take to restore their relationship with God.

Peter responded by telling them what they were lacking and what they must do to obtain God's forgiveness (Acts 2:38). He said they first must repent by changing their hearts toward God's Son.

The need for repentance as a prerequisite to God's forgiveness of sins also was cited in another gospel sermon. Peter said, "Therefore repent and return, so that your sins may be wiped away, in order that times of refreshing may come from the presence of the Lord" (Acts 3:19).

Peter's second command was to "be baptized in the name of Jesus Christ for the forgiveness of your sins; and you shall receive the gift of the Holy Spirit" (Acts 2:38). They were to be born of water and the Spirit to gain entry into the kingdom of God just as Jesus had told Nicodemus in John 3:3–5. Peter further assured them the promise of the Father (which included the blessings of salvation through Jesus) was not only for them, but also their children and all who are far off (Acts 2:39). Those who accepted the Word were baptized and about three thousand souls were added to the saved (Acts 2:41, 47).

This first account of the apostles bringing salvation to the Jews contains all the previously mentioned conditions that Jesus said were necessary for salvation. The Jews believed in Jesus as evidenced by the fact they were pierced to the heart after being taught the gospel message (Acts 2:37). Peter specifically called for them to repent, and after doing so, they complied with Peter's command to be baptized in the name of Jesus Christ for the forgiveness of their sins. Although the text does not explicitly record their confession, it is implied in their submission to baptism in the name of Jesus. Hence, those who responded that day believed, repented, confessed, and were baptized in the name of Jesus, fulfilling all that Jesus required for salvation. Redemption and the steps to acquire it henceforth were made available to all humankind (Acts 2:39).

In Acts 8:5–12, the evangelist Philip began proclaiming Jesus in the city of Samaria. The multitudes were paying close attention to Philip's words because God was affirming the truth of the message by many miraculous signs and wonders. "But when they believed Philip preaching the good news about the kingdom of God and the name of Jesus Christ, they were being baptized, men and women alike" (Acts 8:12).

A similar outcome is recorded for Simon the sorcerer in Acts 8:9–13. He had astonished the people for a long time by performing magic arts. However, upon witnessing the indisputable miracles of God, Simon too believed and was baptized. Here again, we see the affirmation that those who believe and are baptized shall be saved. Belief and baptism are recorded as the first and last steps in the path to salvation (just as Jesus cited in Mark 16:16). Although not explicitly mentioned in this brief summary verse, repentance is required by Jesus as the commitment of an honest heart. Being baptized in the name of Jesus does involve confession.

Yet another salvation account is recorded in Acts 8:26–39. Philip was sent to meet the Ethiopian eunuch—a court official of the queen of the Ethiopians—as he was returning home from

Jerusalem. While the Ethiopian was traveling in his chariot and reading from the prophet Isaiah, Philip approached asking whether he understood the things he was reading. The Ethiopian said, "How could I unless someone guides me?" Then he invited Philip into his chariot to study with him.

Beginning with Isaiah 53:7–8, Philip preached the good news of Jesus. As they were traveling along the road, the Ethiopian spotted a body of water and immediately asked, "What prevents me from being baptized?"

Philip responded: "If you believe with all your heart, you may."

The Ethiopian answered, "I believe that Jesus Christ is the Son of God" (Acts 8:37).

After his confession, they both went down into the water. Philip immersed him, and he came up out of the water to go on his way rejoicing.

What is particularly interesting about this account is that Isaiah 53 contains no reference to baptism. It prophetically speaks of Jesus bearing the sins of many and interceding on behalf of humankind, but it makes no mention of what is required for salvation. That teaching had to come directly from the evangelist Philip through the preaching of the gospel message.

Whatever Philip said must have tied salvation directly to baptism as immersion in water. We know this because the Ethiopian recognized the urgency of acting as soon as he saw a body of water large enough to do the job. Unwilling to wait until arriving back home where he might have been immersed in a local congregation of Christians, he stopped the chariot right then and there and asked to be baptized. He associated his pressing need for salvation directly with the act of being immersed in water. Prior to baptizing the Ethiopian, Philip accepted his confession of belief in Jesus as the Son of God. His repentance is inferred from the request to be baptized (in the name of Jesus) for the forgiveness of his sins. This all took place along a remote desert road (without a large body of church witnesses) in response to hearing the gospel message.

In Acts 9:1–18, we find Luke's account of Saul's conversion. This description is repeated in the words of Paul and recorded in Acts 22:1–16 and Acts 26:1–29. Armed with letters from the high priest, Saul was traveling to Damascus to arrest and persecute Christians. While on his way, he and his associates encountered a bright light from heaven. The voice of Jesus asked Saul why he was persecuting Him. After identifying Himself, Jesus instructed Saul to go to Damascus where it would be told him what he must do (Acts 9:5–6).

Saul was blind and had to be led into Damascus. He spent three days praying and fasting (Acts 9:8–9, 11). In godly sorrow based upon this newfound belief in Jesus, Saul had repented.

Under the Lord's direction, a disciple named Ananias was sent to heal Saul and prepare him to bear the name of Jesus before the Gentiles and kings and the sons of Israel (Acts 9:10–16). When Ananias arrived, he found a devastated man who had come to the realization he had been persecuting the Son of God. Saul was absorbed in prayer and fasting. After healing Saul, Ananias asked, "Now why do you delay? Get up and be baptized, and wash away your sins, calling on His name" (Acts 22:16). Saul responded immediately by being baptized and took food and was strengthened (Acts 9:18–19). From then onward, Saul became known as the apostle Paul (Acts 13:9) and went on to write many of the New Testament letters.

Cornelius and his household were the first Gentiles to receive the gospel message. What makes him so special is prior to this, Jews had no dealings with the Gentiles, and the ministry of Jesus initially was directed only to the "lost sheep of the house of Israel" (Matt. 15:24; John 4:9). Cornelius was a centurion of the Italian cohort who was a devout, God-fearing man, who gave generously to the Jews and prayed to God continually.

Finding favor with God, Cornelius was told in a vision to send for the apostle Peter (Acts 10:1–6). The next day, Peter fell into a trance and had a vision of an object like a great sheet lowered to the ground containing animals unclean under the Jewish Law (Acts 10:9–16). The vision was accompanied by a voice that said, "Get up, Peter, kill and eat" (Acts 10:13). Knowing that Jews were forbidden to eat such animals under the Law of Moses, Peter initially rejected the idea, but the voice proclaimed, "What God has cleansed, no longer consider unholy" (Acts 10:15). The vision ceased after it had been repeated three times, and the messengers of Cornelius showed up at the gate to take Peter back with them.

As Peter was reflecting on what had taken place, the Spirit told him to accompany the messengers without any misgivings about going to the home of a Gentile. When Peter learned about the vision of Cornelius, telling him to send for Peter, the conclusion became obvious: "I most certainly understand now that God is not one to show partiality, but in every nation the man who fears Him and does what is right is welcome to Him" (Acts 10:34–35).

Peter preached the good news of the death, burial, and resurrection of Jesus for the forgiveness of sins to Cornelius and his household (Acts 10:36–43). While Peter was still speaking, the Holy Spirit fell upon these Gentiles, and they began speaking in tongues (i.e., different languages) and exalting God. Upon witnessing the intervention of the Holy Spirit falling on the Gentiles, which had also happened to the apostles on the day of Pentecost, Peter realized that salvation was to be offered to all humankind—Jew and Gentile alike. He ordered the believers to be baptized in the name of Jesus Christ.

This account is unusual because the Holy Spirit fell upon the believers in a miraculous way that empowered them to be able to speak in a different language without any prior instruction. This mimicked what took place with the apostles speaking different languages on the day of Pentecost. Through this miracle, Peter was convinced that God wanted the Gentile believers to be baptized in the name of Jesus just as those Jews were at Pentecost.

Later, Peter was challenged by the Jews living in Jerusalem for what he had done in visiting and baptizing the household of

Cornelius (Acts 11). They even took issue with Peter going to the home of the Gentiles and eating with them. It was only because of the way the Holy Spirit had intervened that Peter was able to argue his case before them. "'Therefore if God gave to them the same gift as He gave to us also after believing in the Lord Jesus Christ, who was I that I could stand in God's way?' When they heard this, they quieted down and glorified God, saying, 'Well then, God has granted to the Gentiles also the repentance that leads to life'" (Acts 11:17–18). These Jewish Christians recognized the significance of what had taken place. They understood that repentance was required of Cornelius and his household prior to baptism and that baptism is what granted them "life" through the saving forgiveness of sins.

In Acts 16:13–15, we have a brief account describing the salvation of Lydia and her household. While searching for a place of prayer, Paul sat down with a group of women and began teaching. Lydia was there with her household. "The Lord opened her heart to respond to the things spoken by Paul" (Acts 16:14). As God opened Lydia's heart, she believed what Paul was teaching about Jesus. Based upon that belief, action was taken because the text says she responded. Verse 15 tells us how she responded; it says she and her household were baptized. Thus we see another salvation process that begins with hearing the gospel message of Jesus, producing belief and ending immediately in baptism for the forgiveness of sins.

The salvation of the Philippian jailer is discussed in Acts 16:25–34. After being arrested and chained in prison, Paul and Silas were praying and singing hymns of praise to God while the other prisoners were listening. Suddenly, there was an earthquake, all the jail doors were opened, and everyone's chains were unfastened. When the jailer awoke and saw all the doors were opened, he drew his sword to kill himself, assuming the prisoners had escaped.

Paul cried out, "Do not harm yourself, for we are all here" (Acts 16:28).

After calling for lights, the jailer brought Paul and Silas out and asked, "Sirs, what must I do to be saved?" (Acts 16:30).

They responded, "Believe in the Lord Jesus, and you will be saved, you and your household" (Acts 16:31).

Paul and Silas confirmed that belief in Jesus would lead to his salvation.

> And they spoke the word of the Lord to him together with all who were in his house. And he took them that very hour of the night and washed their wounds, and immediately he was baptized, he and all his household. (Acts 16:32–33)

In order to believe, the jailer and his family had to be taught, and as a direct result of that teaching, they were all baptized immediately. Once again, we see belief leading to baptism and salvation.

Acts 18:7–11 contains a brief report on the conversion of Crispus and many of the Corinthians. Paul was reasoning in the synagogue every Sabbath, trying to persuade Jews and Greeks. After Silas and Timothy joined him, he devoted himself completely to the task of convincing the Jews that Jesus was the Christ. When they resisted and blasphemed, he moved on to teach the Gentiles. However, "Crispus, the leader of the synagogue, believed in the Lord with all his household, and many of the Corinthians when they heard were believing and being baptized" (Acts 18:8).

Another interesting account is found in Acts 19:1–7. Paul encountered a group of disciples in Ephesus who had been baptized into John's baptism. "Paul asked, 'Did you receive the Holy Spirit when you believed?' And they said to him, 'No, we have not even heard whether there is a Holy Spirit'" (Acts 19:2). By those remarks, it became clear to Paul that they were unfamiliar with the gospel of Jesus and the events that occurred on the day of Pentecost. He explained that John baptized with the baptism of repentance, telling people to believe in Him who was to follow, namely Jesus. "When they heard this, they were baptized in the name of the Lord Jesus" (Acts 19:5).

There are several observations worth making here. First, Paul thought it was important for these disciples to fully understand the gospel message and the role of baptism for their salvation. From the context, it seems likely these disciples had been baptized into John's baptism sometime after the day of Pentecost. The outpouring of the Holy Spirit in fulfillment of the prophecy of Joel did not take place until that time. Likewise, baptism in the name of Jesus was not preached until then. Moreover, aside from two special circumstances—one involving the apostles and another the first Gentile converts—the Holy Spirit was received by believers only after they had repented and been baptized in the name of Jesus (Acts 2:38; 8:14–17). Now, well past that time, these disciples were unfamiliar with baptism in the name of Jesus and receiving the gift of the Holy Spirit. When Paul realized their instruction was incomplete, he taught them correctly. Furthermore, since the age of Christianity had begun, Paul was committed to seeing that these disciples properly complied with God's plan for their salvation. Paul attached particular significance to them being baptized in the name of Jesus. From this passage, we learn salvation depends on fulfilling God's requirement to be immersed in water and doing so with the right heart for the right reason. Anything else is insufficient.

What have we discovered by examining the biblical record of what the inspired apostles and evangelists did to bring salvation to the Jews and Gentiles? Ten conversion accounts have been reviewed from the book of Acts. Although we do not have a detailed record of everything that took place in each instance, we do have a complete representation of the steps involved in salvation. Taken on whole, we found the good news of Jesus being taught to people who believed, repented, confessed, and were baptized by immersion in water. Upon doing so, the text says sins were forgiven and washed away (Acts 2:38; 22:16) and people were saved (Acts 11:14) and rejoiced (Acts 8:8, 39; 16:34). Every conversion account ended immediately in baptism. Nothing that was said or done contradicts the earlier teaching of Jesus or His instructions delivered to the apostles in the Great Commission. In fact, these accounts from the book of Acts confirm the steps to salvation derived from the teachings of Jesus.

In conclusion, we have learned that even though all have missed the mark of being holy as God commanded, it is still possible for us to be forgiven of our shortcomings by claiming the perfect sacrifice of Jesus as the payment for our sins. We claim that gift by:

- believing in Jesus as the Son of God, who died on the cross for our sins and was buried and resurrected from the dead,
- repenting of our sinful lifestyle in godly sorrow turning our heart to pursue God's righteousness and holiness,
- confessing our belief that Jesus is the Son of God who died for our sins, and
- being baptized in the name of Jesus by immersion in water for the forgiveness of sins.

> For the grace of God has appeared, bringing salvation to all men, instructing us to deny ungodliness and worldly desires and to live sensibly, righteously and godly in the present age, looking for the blessed hope and the appearing of the glory of our great God and Savior, Christ Jesus; who gave Himself for us, that He might redeem us from every lawless deed and purify for Himself a people for His own possession, zealous for good deeds. (Titus 2:11–14)

Now, we are in a position to reexamine the three different paths to salvation being taught by those in the world today who profess to be Christians. Recall, these can be summarized in the following ways:

1. First you are baptized—then you are saved—and later you are taught and from that you believe. In this approach, you are baptized and saved without knowing how or why.
2. First you are taught—then you believe—after which you are saved—and later you are baptized. Here baptism has no role in your salvation.
3. First you are taught—then you believe—after which you are baptized—and then you are saved. In this case, baptism serves a definite role that is essential for salvation.

Our goal was to determine which method, if any, is consistent with the ordering in the steps to salvation revealed by the Bible. To build confidence in our conclusion, God's plan of salvation was extracted from the biblical text by examining the scriptures in three different ways looking at:

- what Jesus taught about salvation during His earthly ministry,
- what Jesus commanded His apostles to do in the Great Commission, and
- what the inspired apostles and evangelists actually did and taught to implement God's plan of salvation at the beginning of the Christian Age.

The redundancy associated with conducting three independent studies provides a truth check on our interpretation and result. From all three approaches, we have reached the same conclusion. The good news of the death, burial, and resurrection of Jesus, the Son of God, was taught. Those who heard the Word believed, repented, and confessed their belief in Jesus as the Son of God. Then they were baptized by immersion in water for the forgiveness of their sins and in so doing were saved, redeemed, and restored to fellowship with God. This common result clearly points to the ordering in the third method (belief leads to repentance and confession prior to baptism).

Much of the division and controversy in the religious world that involves God's plan of salvation arises from differences surrounding the nature of belief and baptism. The source of that confusion primarily can be traced to two issues:

1. What does it mean to believe?
2. Why are we baptized?

In chapter 8, we shall address the first of these two questions by examining how the Bible defines a saving belief.

— CHAPTER 8 —

How the Bible Defines a Saving Belief

In chapter 7, we compared the biblical teaching on salvation to the three most commonly held beliefs today among those who profess to be Christians. From that Bible study, we learned that salvation is available to all who are taught the gospel of Jesus Christ and:

- believe in Jesus as the Son of God who saved us through His death, burial, and resurrection,
- repent of a sinful life by a change in heart to follow after a holy God,
- confess their belief in Jesus as our Savior who is the Son of God, and
- are baptized by immersion in water for the forgiveness of sins.

Chapter 8 examines the nature of a saving belief. This concept has led some to teach that salvation is obtained by belief only—without the need for baptism.

To be objective and honest in a study of the Bible, we must acknowledge the existence of many New Testament scriptures that mention salvation with belief but make no reference to repentance, confession, and/or baptism. Consider the following examples:

John 3:16: "For God so loved the world, that He gave His only begotten Son, that whoever believes in Him shall not perish, but have eternal life."

John 3:36: "He who believes in the Son has eternal life; but he who does not obey the Son will not see life, but the wrath of God abides on him."

John 5:24: "Truly, truly, I say to you, he who hears My word, and believes Him who sent Me, has eternal life, and does not come into judgment, but has passed out of death into life."

John 6:40: "For this is the will of My Father, that everyone who beholds the Son and believes in Him will have eternal life, and I Myself will raise him up on the last day."

John 6:47: "Truly, truly, I say to you, he who believes has eternal life."

Acts 10:43: "Of Him all the prophets bear witness that through His name everyone who believes in Him receives forgiveness of sins."

1 John 5:13: "These things I have written to you who believe in the name of the Son of God, so that you may know that you have eternal life."

Do these passages teach that salvation is obtained by belief only without the need for repentance, confession, and baptism? If so, there seems to be a conflict and contradiction among scriptures. From the ministry of Jesus (chapter 6) as well as the evangelistic efforts of the apostles and other inspired preachers (chapter 7), we have identified other specific passages that attest to belief, repentance, confession, and water immersion being required for salvation. However, the aforementioned examples speak of eternal life for believers without mentioning any other conditions. How do we harmonize these scriptures? From the sound learning principles governing Bible study, we know Bible verses cannot conflict with one another since all scripture is inspired by God. That means we must look for a consistent interpretation that acknowledges the truthfulness of all these passages collectively.

Since the issue seems to hinge on the difference between a salvation based on belief as one of several necessary conditions versus a salvation based on belief alone, we shall begin by examining the nature of a saving belief. There are cases in scripture where belief simply means acknowledging something to be true, but is that the belief the inspired writers are referencing in the passages just read? Does a saving belief in Jesus simply mean we accept as truth the fact that Jesus is the Son of God who died for our sins? We know this is false because there are examples in scripture of those who agreed with the fact that Jesus was the Son of God and yet they were neither saved nor accepted by God. In James 2:19, the text reads: "You believe that God is one. You do well; the demons also believe, and shudder."

Demons know God and His Son but have no expectation of salvation. They have what may be called a passive belief. Although a passive belief in Jesus does agree and accept the fact that Jesus is the Son of God, that belief leads nowhere. It is useless, producing no personal response, no change in behavior, no positive outcome, and no commitment. In Matthew 8:28–34, the demons believed but acknowledged their lost fate, crying out, "What business do we have with each other, Son of God? Have You come here to torment us before the time?" James spoke of the inadequacy of having faith in the truth of God without having works or actions to go with it: "For just as the body without the spirit is dead, so also faith without works is dead" (Jas. 2:26).

91

A saving belief is an active belief that produces an outward response, change in mind, change in behavior, and commitment to Jesus.

> Now when He was in Jerusalem at the Passover, during the feast, many believed in His name, observing His signs which He was doing. But Jesus, on His part, was not entrusting Himself to them, for He knew all men, and because He did not need anyone to testify concerning man, for He Himself knew what was in man. (John 2:23–25)

The text clearly states they believed in Jesus because of His miracles, yet Jesus knew their hearts and did not accept them. They had a passive belief that was not going to produce true disciples. These believers did not commit to Jesus, so Jesus did not entrust Himself to them.

> Nevertheless many even of the rulers believed in Him, but because of the Pharisees they were not confessing Him, for fear that they would be put out of the synagogue; for they loved the approval of men rather than the approval of God. (John 12:42–43)

Many of these rulers accepted the truth that Jesus was the Son of God, but according to Matthew 10:32–33, they were not saved because they would not confess the name of Jesus. They were denying Him to keep from being put out of the synagogue.

A belief leading to salvation requires something more than simply accepting the fact that Jesus is the Son of God. "But as many as received Him, to them He gave the right to become children of God, even to those who believe in His name" (John 1:12)

Perhaps this verse provides the greatest insight. By receiving Jesus and believing in His name, Jesus gave them the right and privilege of becoming children of God. They were now eligible. Notice it does not say they were made children of God right then and there. They had met the first necessary condition by accepting Jesus as the Son of God, so salvation through Jesus was now a possibility.

This view is confirmed in John 8:31–32, "So Jesus was saying to those Jews who had believed Him, 'If you continue in My word, then you are truly disciples of Mine; and you will know the truth, and the truth will make you free.'" These Jews believed, but they had not yet been made free from sin. By continuing in His Word, Jesus said they are truly disciples, and because of that, they will come to know the truth, and that truth will make them free from sin (John 8:32–36). Freedom from sin was to occur in the future—provided they continued in the Word where they were to learn the truth about salvation. That truth consists of the other conditions necessary for salvation, namely repentance, confession, and baptism.

There is more to salvation than just accepting or agreeing that Jesus is the Son of God, our Savior. The biblical saving belief referenced by the inspired writers leads us to accept the truth of Jesus as the Son of God, our Savior, and it causes us to respond by taking action based on that belief. It comes with an active commitment to follow Jesus. True believers are saved because they surrender to His will in obedience. The scriptures call this the "obedience of faith."

> Who was declared the Son of God with power by the resurrection from the dead, according to the Spirit of holiness, Jesus Christ our Lord, through whom we have received grace and apostleship to bring about the obedience of faith among all the Gentiles for His name's sake. (Rom. 1:4–5)

> Now to Him who is able to establish you according
> to my gospel and the preaching of Jesus Christ,
> according to the revelation of the mystery which
> has been kept secret for long ages past, but now is
> manifested, and by the scriptures of the prophets,
> according to the commandment of the eternal
> God, has been made known to all the nations,
> leading to obedience of faith. (Rom. 16:25–26)

By using scripture as a commentary on other Bible verses, we see salvation cannot be obtained by simply accepting the fact that Jesus is the Son of God. Our belief must lead us to entrusting ourselves to Him and committing to doing all he has asked us to do. That is the biblical concept of a saving belief, and it explains why Jesus spent time during His ministry talking about other necessary conditions for salvation. Moreover, this definition of belief harmonizes all the previous scriptures.

A saving belief leads to the obedience of faith whereby we are willing to submit to His will. That is what motivates us to comply with the other things Jesus has required of us for salvation. This includes repenting, confessing, and being baptized by immersion in water. Indeed, by having such an active belief, salvation is certain. True believers are saved because they are obedient and have submitted to God's will.

> Although He was a Son, He learned obedience
> from the things which He suffered. And having
> been made perfect, He became to all those who
> obey Him the source of eternal salvation. (Heb.
> 5:8–9)

This verse tells us Jesus provides salvation to all who obey Him. Obedience stems from an active/entrusting belief. In that sense, it is perfectly proper to say true believers have eternal life.

This perspective of how believers have eternal life is identical to the interpretation given to those who love the Lord.

> Listen, my beloved brethren: did not God choose the poor of this world to be rich in faith and heirs of the kingdom which He promised to those who love Him? (Jas. 2:5)

> Blessed is a man who perseveres under trial; for once he has been approved, he will receive the crown of life which the Lord has promised to those who love Him. (Jas. 1:12)

These verses promise that those who love the Lord will receive the crown of life and be heirs of the kingdom. Is this sufficient justification for proposing a doctrine of salvation based on love only? How are we to understand the proper meaning of these promises? We do so by harmonizing these passages with other scriptures. In John 14:15, Jesus says, "If you love Me, you will keep My commandments." We see then that those who love the Lord will keep all His commandments. Those commandments lead to salvation through belief, repentance, confession, and baptism. In the same way, it can be said that those who believe will receive the crown of life and be heirs of the kingdom.

If we attribute salvation to belief only as some suggest, then we are forgiven in the instant we mentally accept the fact that Jesus is the Son of God who died for our sins. That leads to some unusual conclusions. Under such doctrine, repentance, confession, and baptism are not required to have our sins forgiven. In that case, to believe without repenting means we would be living ungodly lives—continuing to sin—and still expect to spend eternity in heaven with God. That denies the problem of sin and contradicts the teachings from Isaiah 59:1–2 and Romans 6:1–2.

If those who believe are saved but must repent immediately

after being saved to stay saved, then salvation must not have been granted in the first place. Without that instant repentance following belief, they are lost all over again. If one must repent and believe in order to be saved, then salvation does not come from belief only. That means belief alone is not sufficient for eternal life; repentance is also needed. This is contrary to the meaning often attributed to the various examples cited at the beginning of the chapter in support of the belief-only doctrine. If that is the case, we must allow the fact that something more than belief is necessary for salvation—namely confession, repentance, and baptism.

Indeed, the Bible does contain other passages directly linking belief to additional conditions for salvation.

Belief and Repentance

Even from His early ministry, we find Jesus commanding all to repent and believe, saying, "The time is fulfilled, and the kingdom of God is at hand; repent and believe in the gospel" (Mark 1:15). Peter said, "Therefore repent and return, so that your sins may be wiped away, in order that times of refreshing may come from the presence of the Lord" (Acts 3:19). Notice that Peter called for people to repent before their sins were forgiven. He made repentance a necessary condition for salvation by proclaiming for them to repent "so that your sins may be wiped away." These times of refreshing were to be granted by God after repentance.

Belief and Confession

Paul linked confession to belief in Romans 10:9, saying, "If you confess with your mouth Jesus as Lord, and believe in your heart that God raised Him from the dead, you will be saved." That confession is made during baptism as seen in the conversion of the Ethiopian eunuch recorded in Acts 8:36–38.

Belief and Baptism

Jesus Himself associated belief with baptism in Mark 16:16, saying, "He who has believed and has been baptized shall be saved."

Through these examples, we have identified separate passages linking and requiring belief and repentance, belief and confession, and belief and baptism. Since all scripture is inspired, all scripture must be true. Collectively, these verses prove a saving belief is one that leads to and is joined inseparably to repentance, confession, and baptism.

Although chapters 6 and 7 document many passages declaring salvation is attained by belief, repentance, confession, and baptism, critics still cling to the belief-only doctrine by appealing to the existence of some verses associating salvation with belief while making no mention of repentance, confession, or baptism. That argument has been addressed by providing a biblical definition of a saving belief. It is an active belief that leads to the obedience of faith, fulfilling all the conditions Jesus cited as necessary for salvation. In that sense, an active belief does equate to eternal life. This understanding allows all the scriptures on salvation to fit together perfectly.

Notice, however, the opposite is not true. If we contend that salvation is obtained by belief only when we accept the fact that Jesus is the Son of God who died for our sins, then we are saved without repentance, confession, and baptism. This doctrine produces the unreasonable conclusions discussed in the previous paragraphs and conflicts with the inspired teaching taken from the ministry of Jesus, the Great Commission, the conversion accounts recorded in the book of Acts, and many teachings found in the New Testament letters. Moreover, these conflicts cannot be resolved.

Another way to arrive at the truth about salvation is to

determine exactly when our sins are forgiven. To do so, we must find scriptures to directly answer that question. Chapter 9 continues the discussion by examining the purpose and meaning of water baptism.

CHAPTER 9
Water Baptism: Its Purpose and Meaning

Chapter 9 is devoted to what the Bible teaches about baptism. Specifically, the focus is on the water baptisms recorded in the New Testament. The initial accounts of baptism are associated with John the Baptist and are mentioned in the first chapters of Mark and John and the third chapters of Matthew and Luke.

From the Greek word employed in the early manuscripts, we know baptism was specified to be a total immersion and not just a sprinkling or pouring. This was discussed thoroughly in chapter 6. The fact that this was an immersion in water also is clear from the text. John openly declared his baptism to be a water baptism in Mark 1:8, Luke 3:16, and John 1:31. A record of John baptizing in the Jordan River is found in Matthew 3:6 and Mark 1:5. Luke's account tells us John began his ministry in response to the Word of the Lord, which came to him (Luke 3:2). John was given the task of preparing the way for the Lord so the nation of Israel would recognize the coming Messiah, whom they awaited (John 1:31). This was in fulfillment of Old Testament prophecies. "'Behold, I am going to send My messenger, and he will clear the way before Me. And the Lord, whom you seek, will suddenly come to His temple; and the messenger of the covenant, in whom you delight, behold, He is coming,' says the LORD of hosts" (Mal. 3:1). "A voice is calling, 'Clear the way for the LORD in the wilderness; Make smooth in the desert a highway for our God'" (Isa. 40:3).

John preached a baptism of repentance for the forgiveness of sins (Mark 1:4; Luke 3:3). It is noteworthy that repentance was required as a condition for baptism. The message John preached was: "Repent, for the kingdom of heaven is at hand" (Matt. 3:2). Moreover, he rebuked the Pharisees and Sadducees when they came for baptism, telling them first to "bear fruit in keeping with repentance" (Matt. 3:8). This was the same message that Jesus preached in His ministry: "Repent, for the kingdom of heaven is at hand" (Matt. 4:17).

It is also important to realize John's baptism was associated with the forgiveness of sins. Paul explained this forgiveness as a shadow of what was to take place through the sacrifice of Jesus to come. "Paul said, 'John baptized with the baptism of repentance, telling the people to believe in Him who was coming after him, that is, in Jesus'" (Acts 19:4).

The forgiveness under John's baptism was obtained by the same power that was able to atone for the sins of Israel under the Old Covenant. It was not by the blood of animal sacrifices for it is impossible for the blood of bulls and goats to take away sins (Heb. 10:4). Instead, it was by the blood of Jesus Christ.

> For this reason He is the mediator of a new covenant, so that, since a death has taken place for the redemption of the transgressions that were committed under the first covenant, those who have been called may receive the promise of the eternal inheritance. (Heb. 9:15)

"For by one offering He has perfected for all time those who are sanctified" (Heb. 10:14).

Even though John's baptism was for the forgiveness of sins, and he called for repentance as a prerequisite to baptism, Jesus asked to be baptized by John. We know Jesus had no need to repent and was guilty of no sin according to 2 Corinthians 5:21 and 1 Peter

2:22. Why did Jesus insist on being baptized? John even tried to prevent it, saying, "I have need to be baptized by You, and do You come to me?" (Matt. 3:14). Jesus provided the answer, saying, "Permit it at this time; for in this way it is fitting for us to fulfill all righteousness" (Matt. 3:15).

A biblical definition of righteousness is provided in Luke 1:6. The text describes it as "walking blamelessly in all the commandments and requirements of the Lord." In this unique case, Jesus was not baptized for the forgiveness of sins but instead to honor the command and desires of the heavenly Father.

In being baptized, Jesus set an example for all of us to follow. He has not asked us to do anything that He Himself was unwilling to do. "For you have been called for this purpose, since Christ also suffered for you, leaving you an example for you to follow in His steps" (1 Pet. 2:21).

> Therefore, He had to be made like His brethren in all things, so that He might become a merciful and faithful high priest in things pertaining to God, to make propitiation for the sins of the people. For since He Himself was tempted in that which He has suffered, He is able to come to the aid of those who are tempted. (Heb. 2:17–18)

> Therefore, since we have a great high priest who has passed through the heavens, Jesus the Son of God, let us hold fast our confession. For we do not have a high priest who cannot sympathize with our weaknesses, but One who has been tempted in all things as we are, yet without sin. (Heb. 4:14–15)

Understanding the significance surrounding the baptism of John prepares the way for us to appreciate the meaning of the baptism Jesus commanded.

What is the purpose of Christian baptism? Why did God command us to be baptized? God does not impose requirements without a reason. In Acts 2:38, the apostle Peter said it was "for the forgiveness of sins." When the Jews realized they were responsible for killing the Christ, the Son of God, they were pierced to the heart and cried out, asking Peter and the apostles, "What shall we do?" They wanted to know what actions or steps they should take to be forgiven and made right with God.

Peter did not tell them they were fine, and nothing was required since they now believed and were pierced in the heart with godly sorrow. No, Peter told them there was something they had yet to do to obtain God's forgiveness. They must repent and then be baptized for the forgiveness of their sins. Just as in John's baptism, we continue to see repentance and immersion in water for the forgiveness of sins. However, here it is performed in the name of Jesus, our Savior. By their obedience in repenting and being baptized as instructed by Peter, God forgave their sins and granted them the gift of the Holy Spirit (Acts 2:38). They were born of water and the Spirit to enter into the kingdom of God (John 3:5).

Based on Peter's later remarks, we know why salvation resides in baptism.

> Who once were disobedient, when the patience of God kept waiting in the days of Noah, during the construction of the ark, in which a few, that is, eight persons, were brought safely through the water. Corresponding to that, baptism now saves you—not the removal of dirt from the flesh, but an appeal to God for a good conscience—through the resurrection of Jesus Christ. (1 Pet. 3:20–21 NASB)

Peter is referencing Noah's family as they were brought to safety in the ark as the evil was washed off the face of the earth by the Great Flood waters. He makes an analogy to the cleansing achieved in water baptism as he says: "Corresponding to that baptism now saves you" (v. 21).

Peter declares that we are saved during the actual act of baptism. This is entirely consistent with what Peter commanded in Acts 2:38 when he called for them to be baptized for the forgiveness of sins. Since sins are forgiven during baptism, it is perfectly proper to claim that baptism brings salvation. Anticipating the confusion with a physical cleansing, Peter quickly clarifies by stating we are not saved by the removal of dirt from the flesh. The significance of baptism has nothing to do with the physical hygiene of washing in water. Instead, something spiritual is taking place during this physical act. Peter went on to say the power to save actually comes "through the resurrection of Jesus Christ" (not the water).

So, how does being baptized link us to the resurrection of Jesus Christ? In this literal translation of the Greek (formal equivalence), Peter says baptism is the way we appeal to God for a good conscience. The text also might be translated to petition for a good conscience. By our obedience of faith in being baptized, we are actually calling on the name of the Lord, making a formal appeal to God for forgiveness through the death, burial, and resurrection of Jesus Christ.

In being immersed in water, our consciences are cleared by the knowledge we have been granted forgiveness of sins. This picture of baptism is reinforced by the teachings of the apostle Paul:

> Or do you not know that all of us who have been
> baptized into Christ Jesus have been baptized into
> his death? Therefore, we have been buried with
> Him through baptism into death, so that as Christ
> was raised from the dead through the glory of the
> Father, so we too might walk in newness of life.
> (Rom. 6:3–4)

Paul explains that being baptized into the name of Jesus means we are being baptized into His death. Just as Jesus was resurrected from the dead, we leave the old sinful self under the waters of baptism and rise out of the water to a newness of life—a fresh start, a new life cleansed from sin.

> For if we have become united with Him in the likeness of His death, certainly we shall also be in the likeness of His resurrection, knowing this, that our old self was crucified with Him, in order that our body of sin might be done away with, so that we would no longer be slaves to sin; for he who has died is freed from sin. Now if we have died with Christ, we believe that we shall also live with Him. (Rom. 6:5–8)

We are united with Jesus in a death like His during our baptism where we are baptized into His death. In baptism, God has given us a physical representation of the death, burial, and resurrection of Jesus. By our reenactment, in going down under the water and rising again, we are united with Him in death, spiritually putting the sinful old self to death so we can rise up out of the water free from sin. What a beautiful image God has given to us.

God has appealed to our dual natures by using a physical event to help us understand the far deeper spiritual cleansing that is taking place for salvation. Paul says our resurrection to life and our freedom from sin are conditional. We possess these spiritual blessings if we have been united with Him in a death like His (Rom. 6:5) and if we have died with Christ (Rom. 6:8). That union and death occur in our baptism.

> Or do you not know that all of us who have been baptized into Christ Jesus have been baptized into his death? Therefore we have been buried with

A DEBT I CANNOT PAY

Him through baptism into death, so that as Christ
was raised from the dead through the glory of the
Father, so we too might walk in newness of life.
(Rom. 6:3–4)

Hebrews supplies additional commentary and support for the
teachings of 1 Peter 3:20–21.

> Therefore, brethren, since we have confidence to
> enter the holy place by the blood of Jesus, by a
> new and living way which He inaugurated for us
> through the veil, that is, His flesh, and since we
> have a great priest over the house of God, let us
> draw near with a sincere heart in full assurance of
> faith, having our hearts sprinkled clean from an
> evil conscience and our bodies washed with pure
> water. (Heb. 10:19–22)

Notice the parallel between these passages. We are able to draw
near to God by the cleansing blood of Jesus that was offered in the
sacrifice of our mediator and great priest on the cross of Calvary
(Heb. 10:19). How are we able to approach the throne of God with
a sincere heart in full assurance of faith? We do so by having our
hearts sprinkled clean from an evil conscience and our bodies
washed with pure water (Heb. 10:22).

We are able to enter the holy place in full assurance of faith
by the blood of Jesus after our hearts are sprinkled clean during
the washing of our bodies with water in baptism. Here we learn
that we encounter the saving blood sacrifice of Jesus in the water
of baptism as we are buried with Him in a likeness of His death.

Notice the similarity in words that describe what takes place
during baptism. The text from Peter calls it an appeal to God for a
good conscience. The Hebrew writer calls it a cleansing of an evil
conscience. Moreover, Hebrews 9:14 tells us the blood of Christ

cleanses our conscience from dead works. The consistency among these passages is clear teaching that baptism defines the moment when our sins are forgiven. That is why baptism is essential for salvation, and it explains why Jesus commanded it.

There also is convincing support for the necessity of baptism found in the conversion of Saul. After being blinded during his encounter with Jesus on the road to Damascus, Saul was told to go into the city where it would be told him what he must do (Acts 9:6). In his heartfelt remorse over the persecution of Jesus and His followers, Saul spent three days fasting and in prayer—taking neither food nor drink (Acts 9:9, 11).

Even though Saul believed in Jesus, had a heart of sorrow and repentance, and was granted healing through God's messenger Ananias, Saul was still lost in sin. Ananias said, "Now why do you delay? Get up and be baptized, and wash away your sins, calling on His name" (Acts 22:16). By asking Saul why he was delaying, Ananias was indicating that something more needed to be done. Even though Saul had been healed, he was still lacking. Salvation had not yet been achieved. He was still in sin. To remedy that, Ananias commanded Saul to be baptized and to wash away his sins by calling on His name. This account exemplifies the teaching found in 1 Peter 3:20–21 and Hebrews 10:19–22.

Baptism was required for Saul's salvation even though he had believed and repented. Ananias said that by being baptized Saul's sins would be washed away. This involved having his heart sprinkled clean from an evil conscience and his body washed with pure water (Heb. 10:22). Ananias also said that, in baptism, Saul was calling on the name of Jesus. Clearly, Ananias recognized baptism as an appeal to God for a good conscience (1 Pet. 3:21).

In his later ministry, Saul (by then known as Paul) taught these same things.

If you confess with your mouth Jesus as Lord, and believe in your heart that God raised Him from the dead, you will be saved; for with the heart a person believes, resulting in righteousness, and with the mouth he confesses, resulting in salvation. (Rom. 10:9–10)

Salvation indeed will come to a believer who confesses Jesus as Lord. That is exactly what happened to the Ethiopian in Acts 8:36–38 when he confessed Jesus as the Son of God at his baptism. Paul said, "For whoever will call on the name of the Lord will be saved" (Rom. 10:13). That call upon the name of the Lord is executed during baptism. It is our appeal to God for a good conscience (1 Pet. 3:21).

In his preaching, Paul reminded the Corinthians that many had been guilty of grossly unrighteous behavior but now they were cleansed.

Such were some of you; but you were washed, but you were sanctified, but you were justified in the name of the Lord Jesus Christ and in the Spirit of our God. (1 Cor. 6:11)

Just like Paul, they were washed and sanctified by baptism in the name of Jesus while calling on the name of the Lord.

The essential need for baptism in the overall plan of God is further evident in Paul's teaching to the Galatian Christians.

For you are all sons of God through faith in Christ Jesus. For all of you who were baptized into Christ have clothed yourselves with Christ. There is neither Jew nor Greek, there is neither slave nor free man, there is neither male nor female; for you are all one in Christ Jesus. And if you belong to Christ, then you are Abraham's descendants, heirs according to promise. (Gal. 3:26–29)

We become sons of God and demonstrate our faith in Christ Jesus by clothing ourselves with Christ. According to these verses, we get into Christ and are clothed with Him by being baptized into His name (v. 27). Our baptism is what unites us all as one in Christ Jesus (v. 28), and if we have been baptized into Christ, then we are heirs. This fulfills the promise of Genesis 12:3 where God told Abraham: "And in you all the families of the earth shall be blessed."

Occasionally, baptism is wrongly thought of as a work that is done by a believer to earn salvation. Nothing could be further from the truth. In fact, such a strategy was shown to fail in chapter 5 where potential solutions to the problem of sin were discussed. Since sin is what separates us from God, according to Isaiah 59:1–2, the only way for us to secure our own salvation would be to lead a perfect, sinless life and never lose it in the first place. That, of course, is impossible since everyone has sinned and fallen short of the glory of God (Rom. 3:23). Moreover, good works do not remove the guilt and conviction of a lawbreaker. This is true even in our secular judicial system. Lawbreaking must have consequences to preserve justice and righteousness. There is no path to salvation by performing good works to earn eternal life.

The Bible clearly teaches that we are saved by God's grace through our faith in God.

> But God, being rich in mercy, because of His great love with which He loved us, even when we were dead in our transgressions, made us alive together with Christ (by grace you have been saved), and raised us up with Him, and seated us with Him in the heavenly places in Christ Jesus, so that in the ages to come He might show the surpassing riches of His grace in kindness toward us in Christ Jesus. (Eph. 2:4–7)

Moreover, salvation is the gift of God to humankind.

> For by grace you have been saved through faith;
> and that not of yourselves, it is the gift of God;
> not as a result of works, so that no one may boast.
> (Eph. 2:8–9)

By definition, gifts are never earned. However, we must agree to either accept a gift or reject it. God does not force salvation upon us. That would violate our free will and amount to a free pass for our sins. To receive the gift of salvation, we still must claim it. That is done by having faith in the promise of God to save us when we comply with His will by believing, repenting, confessing, and being baptized to appeal for the forgiveness of sins. This is our obedience of faith (Rom 1:5; 16:26).

Even if baptism is called some kind of work, it certainly is not a work done by the believer. In baptism, believers allow someone else to immerse them in water. The person being baptized is totally passive and submissive in the process. There is no work whatsoever being done by the recipient of baptism. They are claiming God's gift by allowing themselves to be immersed into the death of Jesus. According to God's Word, we contact the sacrificial blood of Christ and claim the precious gift of salvation by calling on the name of the Lord in baptism.

The Bible does, in fact, speak of a work being accomplished during baptism, but it is a work being done by God. In Colossians 2, Paul encourages the Christians to walk in Christ Jesus, firmly rooted, being built up and established in the faith just as they were instructed (Col. 2:6–7). In context, Paul was concerned that men may delude them with persuasive arguments (Col. 2:4). He issued warnings about the threat to their faith.

> See to it that no one takes you captive through
> philosophy and empty deception, according to

the tradition of men, according to the elementary principles of the world, rather than according to Christ. For in Him all the fullness of Deity dwells in bodily form, and in Him you have been made complete, and He is the head over all rule and authority. (Col. 2:8–10)

Paul discusses their spiritual cleansing through the sacrifice of Jesus Christ:

And in Him you were also circumcised with a circumcision made without hands, in the removal of the body of the flesh by the circumcision of Christ; having been buried with Him in baptism, in which you were also raised up with Him through faith in the working of God, who raised Him from the dead. (Col. 2:11–12)

Paul speaks of a spiritual circumcision in Christ. It is not a physical cutting of flesh made with hands. Instead, he speaks of a removal of the body of the sins of the flesh. He goes on to specify who has undergone this spiritual circumcision. It is those who have been buried with Him in baptism through which they were also raised up with Him (v. 12). Furthermore, this was done through faith in the working of God, who raised Jesus from the dead.

There are two very important points to be made from this text. First, the text states baptism is an act of faith on the part of the believer—faith in God's spiritual circumcision and removing the body of sins created by our fleshly pursuits. This is our forgiveness by being washed in the blood of Christ. Second, there is work being done in baptism, but it is the work of God. It is He who is doing the work. God is forgiving our sins. He is performing a spiritual circumcision. If there is any confusion over what is being said here, it is removed by Paul's next statement: "When you were dead in your transgressions and the uncircumcision of your flesh, He made you alive together with Him, having forgiven us all our transgressions" (Col. 2:13). Paul equates being dead in transgressions with an uncircumcised state. Being alive together with Christ comes from having sins forgiven and that spiritual circumcision is said to take place during baptism (Col. 2:11–12).

Many other passages link baptism to the forgiveness of sins.

> Husbands, love your wives, just as Christ also loved the church and gave Himself up for her, so that He might sanctify her, having cleansed her by the washing of water with the word, that He might present to Himself the church in all her glory, having no spot or wrinkle or any such thing; but that she would be holy and blameless. (Eph. 5:25–27)

The church is the body of Christ (Eph. 1:22–23), and Christ gave Himself up for the sanctification of the church, making her holy and blameless. That cleansing was performed by the washing of water with the Word. In Christianity, the only washing of water associated with sanctification is baptism! Moreover, at the time Paul wrote this letter, he said there was only one baptism (Eph. 4:5), and it was the water immersion commanded by Jesus.

> But when the kindness of God our Savior and His love for humankind appeared, He saved us, not on the basis of deeds which we have done in righteousness, but according to His mercy, by the washing of regeneration and renewing by the Holy Spirit, whom He poured out upon us richly through Jesus Christ our Savior, so that being justified by His grace we would be made heirs according to the hope of eternal life. (Titus 3:4–7)

Salvation does not come from righteous deeds or works to earn our salvation. Rather, it comes from God's grace and mercy through two things:

- the washing of regeneration
- the renewing by the Holy Spirit

Where and how are these two things realized? The washing of regeneration for salvation is baptism (1 Pet. 3:21; Acts 22:16, Eph. 5:26), and the gift of the Holy Spirit likewise is granted from baptism (Acts 2:38). Recall the commands of Peter in Acts 2:38, "Repent, and each of you be baptized in the name of Jesus Christ for the forgiveness of your sins; and you will receive the gift of the Holy Spirit." Indeed, we must be born of water and the Spirit to enter into the kingdom of God (John 3:5).

The apostle Paul said, "Blessed be the God and Father of our Lord Jesus Christ, who has blessed us with every spiritual blessing in the heavenly places in Christ" (Eph. 1:3). This tells us all spiritual blessing reside in Christ, including our forgiveness of sins and salvation (Eph. 1:7; 2 Tim. 2:10).

We enter into Christ by being baptized.

> For all of you who were baptized into Christ have clothed yourselves with Christ. There is neither Jew nor Greek, there is neither slave nor free man, there is neither male nor female; for you are all one in Christ Jesus. And if you belong to Christ, then you are Abraham's descendants, heirs according to promise. (Gal. 3:27–29)

By now, it should be clear that baptism is essential for our salvation. It represents the final step in claiming the sacrifice of Jesus as the payment for our sins. In being baptized into His death, we appeal to God for a good conscience and contact the saving blood of Jesus to rise a new creature—holy and pure.

Make no mistake. The journey of a believer does not end at baptism. It is only the beginning. Equally important is what comes next. Chapter 10 closes the book by considering what is involved in living as a disciple of Jesus.

CHAPTER 10
Living as a Disciple of Jesus

In the final chapter, we begin by reviewing what has been covered thus far. We have seen that an eternal, all-present, all-knowing, all-powerful Spirit Being called God willed into existence the space, matter, and energy that make up our physical universe. In so doing, He established the beginning of time itself. Distinct from all other living creatures, God created humankind in His own image, granting us an eternal spirit in addition to a physical body of flesh and blood. By God's design, you are special—and you must never forget that.

In the beginning, the first couple was created to be holy and pure, conforming to the same goodness and character of God. They were intended to live in perfect harmony and fellowship with the Creator. However, when Adam and Eve chose to disobey God's command, they missed the mark and sinned, creating a spiritual barrier that separated them from a holy and just God. That same tendency to reject God and disobey His commands has produced a sin problem for all of us today. Being guilty of breaking God's laws, we too have severed our relationship with Him. Left in that state, we are lost, risking eternal separation from God in hell when our physical lives end. That is the problem of sin.

Because God loves us, He does not want anyone to remain lost in that dismal state. However, the response of a holy God is limited. Because He is just, righteous, and holy, He cannot have fellowship with lawbreakers or unconditionally forgive our sins. The only way out is through Jesus, the Son of God, who was born as flesh and blood to live a perfect life, revealing God's will for humankind and ultimately offering Himself as a substitute by taking the punishment for our sins.

Jesus is God's solution to the problem of sin, and there is none other. Through God's plan of salvation, we have a way to claim the sacrifice of Jesus as the payment for our sins. By His gift to us, our debt can be paid, and we can be redeemed and brought back into full fellowship with God. Being restored to holiness, we have the promise of eternal life in heaven with Him when our physical existence ends.

Although salvation is a gift to us, we still must claim it. God does not force Himself on anyone. To embrace the gift of salvation, we must:

- believe in Jesus as the Son of God who died for our sins and was resurrected in a victory over death,
- repent, changing our hearts to pursue righteousness and a life of holiness,
- confess our faith in Jesus as the Son of God, our Savior, and
- be baptized by immersion in water for the forgiveness of our sins.

After baptism, we become true disciples of Jesus Christ—free from the bonds of sin. In the remainder of chapter 10, we shall examine what comes next in the life of a baptized believer.

When believers are baptized for the forgiveness of sins, they are added to the Lord's church. The word *church* comes from a translation of a Greek word meaning "the called out." The association of the church with the called out is entirely appropriate since Jesus said, "I have not come to call the righteous but sinners to repentance" (Luke 5:32). We are, therefore, being called out of sin into the kingdom of God. This formed the basis for the early ministry of John the Baptist and Jesus as they called for all to repent, proclaiming the kingdom of heaven is at hand. Acts 2:41 tells us how people gained entry into the church: "So then, those who had received his word were baptized; and that day there were added about three thousand souls."

By whom and to what were these baptized believers added? Acts 2:47 says, "And the Lord was adding to their number day by day those who were being saved." Baptized believers were added to the number of those who were being saved (having their sins forgiven). The Lord Himself added them to the number being saved.

Our salvation does not depend on the approval of any religious group of individuals. That control belongs exclusively to Jesus, and admission is granted when we submit to God's plan for our salvation.

The fact that the church is populated by those being saved is clear from Paul's instruction to the Ephesians:

> Husbands, love your wives, just as Christ also loved the church and gave Himself up for her, so that He might sanctify her, having cleansed her by the washing of water with the word, that He might present to Himself the church in all her glory, having no spot or wrinkle or any such thing; but that she would be holy and blameless. (Eph. 5:25–27)

Paul is teaching husbands to love their wives as Christ loves the church. Notice what Paul said Christ did for the church. Jesus gave Himself up for the church to sanctify the body. Furthermore, that body was cleansed by the washing of water—a reference to baptism. What resulted was a group of people who were sanctified, holy, and blameless. They were free from sin. The members of the church are those who have been saved.

The church is called the body of Christ, and Jesus is the sole head of that body.

> And He put all things in subjection under His feet, and gave Him as head over all things to the church, which is His body, the fullness of Him who fills all in all. (Eph.1:22–23)

> He is also head of the body, the church; and He is the beginning, the firstborn from the dead, so that He Himself will come to have first place in everything. (Col. 1:18)

From these two passages, it is clear that the body of Christ is the church. It is His body because He purchased it with His own blood (1 Pet. 1:18–19). Since the body belongs to Jesus, He is the head of the church. That means all spiritual authority rests with Jesus, and church doctrine, membership, and worship practices are under His control. We must learn God's expectations by studying the Bible. Men, women, councils, or other earthly organizations are not the head of the body.

The Bible refers to the members of the church by different names. In Acts 11:26, they were called Christians first at Antioch. They also frequently are called saints (Acts 9:13; 26:10; Rom. 1:6–7; 2 Cor. 1:1; Eph. 1:1). The biblical use of this word does not make any distinction among the saved members of the body of Christ. All Christians are saints. We know this because the apostle Paul provided the definition of a saint:

> Paul, called as an apostle of Jesus Christ by the will of God, and Sosthenes our brother, To the church of God which is at Corinth, to those who have been sanctified in Christ Jesus, saints by calling, with all who in every place call on the name of

our Lord Jesus Christ, their Lord and ours. (1 Cor. 1:1–2)

Paul addresses this letter to the Church at Corinth and then specifies who these people are. They are those who have been sanctified in Christ Jesus—saints by calling. Paul defines saints as Christians who have been sanctified in Christ Jesus (made holy by being cleansed of their sins). That sanctification occurred in their baptism. Biblically, saints are the sanctified members of Christ's church.

It is important to realize, by God's design, there is only one church. When the Bible speaks of churches in the plural sense, it is not referring to different factions of followers but rather different congregations that are part of the same universal body of saved believers who happen to assemble in different locations. Paul and the brethren with him wrote the book of Galatians "to the churches of Galatia" (Gal. 1:2). Similarly, 2 Corinthians 8:1 says, "Now, brethren, we wish to make known to you the grace of God which has been given in the churches of Macedonia." Romans 16:16 reads, "Greet one another with a holy kiss. All the churches of Christ greet you."

Paul's writings reflect his desire for unity in the church:

> Now may the God who gives perseverance and encouragement grant you to be of the same mind with one another according to Christ Jesus, so that with one accord you may with one voice glorify the God and Father of our Lord Jesus Christ. (Rom. 15:5–6)

Paul admonished the Ephesian Christians to walk in a manner worthy of their calling.

> Being diligent to preserve the unity of the Spirit in the bond of peace. There is one body and one

Spirit, just as also you were called in one hope of
your calling; one Lord, one faith, one baptism, one
God and Father of all who is over all and through
all and in all. (Eph. 4:3–6)

This passage may provide the clearest picture of Christian unity
in the entire Bible. Paul commands these Christians to be diligent
to preserve the unity of the Spirit. He then goes on to list what
Christians are to unite around. First on that list is the concept of
"one body" or "one church." Also mentioned are one Spirit, one
hope, one Lord, one faith, one baptism, and one God and Father
who is over all. Note the extraordinary emphasis placed on the
quantity "one."

When Jesus poured out His heart in the prayer of John 17,
He was well aware of the coming threats of division through the
apostasy whereby believers would fall away from the word of truth.
Jesus acknowledged that He had taught His apostles the words
from the Father and that they had believed and accepted them
(John 17:6–8). He went on to ask the Father to "keep them in
Your name, the name which You have given Me, that they may be
one, even as We are" (John 17:11), emphasizing the need for unity.

Jesus called for their sanctification in the truth of the Word
(John 17:17). That prayer was expanded to include those who
believe through the words of the apostles.

I do not ask on behalf of these alone, but for those
also who believe in Me through their word. (John
17:20)

That they may all be one; even as You, Father, are
in Me and I in You, that they also may be in Us,
so that the world may believe that You sent Me.
(John 17:21)

Here we see the importance of unity in the church. Jesus said unity is needed so the world may believe "You sent me." Our unity is what adds credibility to the Son of God and the inspiration of the gospel message. When we project the image of a divided church, our differences become a stumbling block to the lost souls of the world who are watching and listening. Religious division can cause people to question the authenticity of the message and the messenger:

- Is this a true revelation from God or just a man-made tradition?
- How can anyone ever hope to understand all this?
- Are any of these teachings really binding?

Such needless confusion undermines our ability to save lost souls, especially on the mission field where innocents are confronted by different religious names, doctrines, worship practices, and plans of salvation. In John 17:22, Jesus said the glory He received from the Father was passed to His apostles "that they may be one, just as We are one." In verse 23, Jesus pleaded for unity a fourth time saying, "I in them and You in Me, that they may be perfected in unity, so that the world may know that You sent Me, and loved them, even as You have loved Me." As Jesus faced His death on the cross, His most urgent petition to the Father was for the apostles and all who believe through their words to be united just as the Father and Son are one.

A quick view of the religious world today reveals unity is not the case. Many so-called Christian churches are divided by name, founder, origin, organization, doctrine, sources of authority, traditions, worship practices, membership, works, and even plans of salvation. These differences have produced the Catholic Church, the Eastern Orthodox Church, Protestant denominations, and many factions and cults, all professing to be followers of Christ—yet deviating from the one church described in the books of the New Testament. How can this be when the Bible directly reveals God's plea for Christian unity?

The apostle Paul provided some insight in his warning to the Ephesian elders.

> Be on guard for yourselves and for all the flock, among which the Holy Spirit has made you overseers, to shepherd the church of God which He purchased with His own blood. I know that after my departure savage wolves will come in among you, not sparing the flock; and from among your own selves men will arise, speaking perverse things, to draw away the disciples after them. (Acts 20:28–30)

When through arrogance, people seek to build a following by exercising their own authority in place of the God's will, the outcome is apostasy and division.

So, how can Christians achieve and maintain unity? By accepting the Bible as the sole source for all spiritual authority and adhering to the inspired teachings and examples provided for our guidance and learning.

> Whoever speaks, is to do so as one who is speaking the utterances of God; whoever serves is to do so as one who is serving by the strength which God supplies; so that in all things God may be glorified through Jesus Christ, to whom belongs the glory and dominion forever and ever. Amen. (1 Pet. 4:11)

We must speak and act based on the authority of God—not men. That authority comes only from the inspired words of the Bible where it is transmitted to us by commands, inspired examples, and sound/necessary inferences. Moreover, all that we do must glorify God through Jesus Christ. Unity cannot exist until everyone is willing to submit themselves to God's pattern and design for the Lord's church. Just because we think our way is acceptable, does not make it so.

> "For My thoughts are not your thoughts, Nor are your ways My ways," declares the LORD. "For as the heavens are higher than the earth, So are My ways higher than your ways And My thoughts than your thoughts." (Isa. 55:8–9)

We are incapable of going it alone, "I know, O Lord, that a man's way is not in himself, Nor is it in a man who walks to direct his steps" (Jer. 10:23). When we act based on our own conscience, we risk disaster. Proverbs 16:25 warns, "There is a way which seems right to a man, But its end is the way of death."

Our obligation as Christians is to be a part of the one true church described in the pages of the New Testament. Jesus Himself warned us not to follow the masses seeking an alternate way to eternal life.

> Enter through the narrow gate; for the gate is wide and the way is broad that leads to destruction, and there are many who enter through it. For the gate is small and the way is narrow that leads to life, and there are few who find it. (Matt. 7:13–14).

Being a Christian and member of Christ's church does not mean we will never sin. Christians, after all, are human and still struggle with temptations and poor decisions. Just like infants, new converts must grow spiritually and learn how to live as disciples of Christ.

Try as we may, all will miss the mark and fall short of the glory of God from time to time (Rom. 3:23). The apostle John said, "If we say that we have no sin, we are deceiving ourselves and the truth is not in us" (1 John 1:8).

Given the certainty of sinning, what is a Christian to do? Is baptism required all over again? No. John said, "My little children, I am writing these things to you so that you may not sin. And if anyone sins, we have an Advocate with the Father, Jesus Christ the righteous" (1 John 2:1). In 1 Timothy 2:5, Paul reminds Christians, "For there is one God, and one mediator also between God and men, the man Christ Jesus."

Christians have a personal advocate and mediator to God, the Father.

> If we confess our sins, He is faithful and righteous to forgive us our sins and to cleanse us from all unrighteousness. (1 John 1:9)

That assurance is available only if we continue as faithful followers of Jesus.

> If we say that we have fellowship with Him and yet walk in the darkness, we lie and do not practice the truth; if we walk in the Light as He Himself is in the Light, we have fellowship with one another, and the blood of Jesus His Son cleanses us from all sin. (1 John 1:6–7)

Christians who live for God and walk in His light are assured forgiveness by the cleansing blood of Jesus when they repent and confess their sins to Him.

It is still possible for a believer who once was baptized to fall away and be lost for eternity. That comes from rejecting God to walk in darkness and pursue worldly lusts.

If we say that we have fellowship with Him and yet walk in the darkness, we lie and do not practice the truth. (1 John 1:6)

A Christian cannot claim to have fellowship with God while walking in darkness. John called that a lie—contrary to the truth. If we no longer have fellowship with God, that separation leads to spiritual death.

John cautioned against being seduced by worldly things.

Do not love the world nor the things in the world. If anyone loves the world, the love of the Father is not in him. For all that is in the world, the lust of the flesh and the lust of the eyes and the boastful pride of life, is not from the Father, but is from the world. The world is passing away, and also its lusts; but the one who does the will of God lives forever. (1 John 2:15–17)

One who chooses lusts is walking in the darkness and part of a world that is passing away. The one who walks in the light and does the will of the Father lives forever.

The Bible is filled with many admonitions that encourage Christians to remain faithful. Christians are expected to live as disciples of Jesus, walking in the light to the end of their days.

If a Christian returns to the defilements of the world, the latter state is worse than never having become a Christian.

For if, after they have escaped the defilements of the world by the knowledge of the Lord and Savior Jesus Christ, they are again entangled in them and are overcome, the last state has become worse for them than the first. For it would be better for them not to have known the way of righteousness, than having known it, to turn away from the holy commandment handed on to them. It has happened to them according to the true proverb, "A dog returns to its own vomit," and "A sow, after washing, returns to wallowing in the mire." (2 Pet. 2:20–22)

For in the case of those who have once been enlightened and have tasted of the heavenly gift and have been made partakers of the Holy Spirit, and have tasted the good Word of God and the powers of the age to come, and then have fallen away, it is impossible to renew them again to repentance, since they again crucify to themselves the Son of God and put Him to open shame. For ground that drinks the rain which often falls on it and brings forth vegetation useful to those for whose sake it is also tilled, receives a blessing from God; but if it yields thorns and thistles, it is worthless and close to being cursed, and it ends up being burned. (Heb. 6:4–8)

For a Christian, returning to a life of sin is the same as trampling underfoot the sacrifice of Jesus on the cross. Verses 7 and 8 make an analogy contrasting the ground that bears useful vegetation with ground that yields only thorns and thistles. The fertile ground represents faithful Christians who prosper. The ground producing thorns and thistles is worthless and ends up being burned and destroyed. So it is with a life that has fallen away into darkness.

Jesus referenced something similar to Hebrews 6:7–8 in the parable of the sower found in Luke 8:5–14. The seed that fell on the rocky soil grew up and withered away, representing those who fell away in times of temptation. The seed falling in thorns grew up and was choked out, describing those who were overcome with worries, riches, and pleasures of life (thereby bearing no fruit).

Even the apostle Paul had to work to control his body and keep from losing the prize of salvation and being disqualified.

> Everyone who competes in the games exercises self-control in all things. They then do it to receive a perishable wreath, but we an imperishable. Therefore I run in such a way, as not without aim; I box in such a way, as not beating the air; but I discipline my body and make it my slave, so that, after I have preached to others, I myself will not be disqualified. (1 Cor. 9:25–27)

> Now I make known to you, brethren, the gospel which I preached to you, which also you received, in which also you stand, by which also you are saved, if you hold fast the word which I preached to you, unless you believed in vain. (1 Cor. 15:1–2)

The gospel message is able to save—if you hold fast the Word. That means embrace it, accept it, and live it. Those who do not hold fast are said to have believed in vain (without the benefit of salvation).

John wrote to the Church in Ephesus.

> Do not fear what you are about to suffer. Behold, the devil is about to cast some of you into prison, so that you will be tested, and you will have tribulation for ten days. Be faithful until death, and I will give you the crown of life. (Rev. 2:10)

The crown of life was to be awarded to those who were faithful until death.

The key point is to remember that having our sins forgiven by becoming Christians does not mean our journeys are over. It is merely the beginning of a new life in holiness. Our lives are intended to glorify God and bring others to salvation through Jesus. The ability to serve as a faithful disciple of Jesus Christ depends on knowing how to live as a Christian and maintaining the strength and commitment to do so. This is an important part of the spiritual growth that is to follow salvation.

Recall the words of Jesus spoken to the apostles:

> Go therefore and make disciples of all the nations, baptizing them in the name of the Father and the Son and the Holy Spirit, teaching them to observe all that I commanded you; and lo, I am with you always, even to the end of the age. (Matt. 28:19–20)

Jesus commanded His apostles to make disciples by baptizing them and then teaching them to observe all that He had commanded them. Christians must be taught the whole truth revealed by God. This includes being saved, living for Christ, and walking in the light. That is the task of a lifetime.

For us today, that knowledge comes from the Bible.

> All scripture is inspired by God and profitable for teaching, for reproof, for correction, for training in righteousness; so that the man of God may be adequate, equipped for every good work. (2 Tim. 3:16–17)

We are expected to feed on the Word of God.

> Be diligent to present yourself approved to God as a workman who does not need to be ashamed,

accurately handling the word of truth. (2 Tim. 2:15)

The Hebrew writer pointed out the expectations and advantages of spiritual growth and maturity.

> For though by this time you ought to be teachers, you have need again for someone to teach you the elementary principles of the oracles of God, and you have come to need milk and not solid food. For everyone who partakes only of milk is not accustomed to the word of righteousness, for he is an infant. But solid food is for the mature, who because of practice have their senses trained to discern good and evil. (Heb. 5:12–14)

We are expected to grow in our knowledge of God to be equipped to teach others. By putting that knowledge to work in our lives, we train our senses to discern between good and evil. That spiritual maturity equips us to lead faithful Christian lives, overcoming the temptations of the world.

God has shown us the path to a better life. It is one that brings hope, love, and joy—and it is freely available to all.

> For the grace of God has appeared, bringing salvation to all men, instructing us to deny ungodliness and worldly desires and to live sensibly, righteously and godly in the present age, looking for the blessed hope and the appearing of the glory of our great God and Savior, Christ Jesus; who gave Himself for us, that He might redeem us from every lawless deed and purify for Himself a people for His own possession, zealous for good deeds. (Titus 2:11–14)

It is appropriate to end with the words of Jesus taken from Matthew 7:24–27:

> Therefore everyone who hears these words of Mine and acts on them, may be compared to a wise man who built his house on the rock. And the rain fell, and the floods came, and the winds blew and slammed against that house; and yet it did not fall, for it had been founded on the rock. Everyone who hears these words of Mine and does not act on them, will be like a foolish man who built his house on the sand. The rain fell, and the floods came, and the winds blew and slammed against that house; and it fell—and great was its fall.

If you have not claimed the gift of eternal life by becoming a Christian, what better time than now? Please don't delay. "For what does it profit a man to gain the whole world, and forfeit his soul?" (Mark 8:36). "He who has ears, let him hear" (Matt. 13:9).